ATHENA

Athena was among the most widely worshipped of the ancient Greek deities. Chiefly associated with Athens, she was also venerated through- out the cities and regions of the Greek world where her principal role was the guardian of the *polis*, the principal organisation unit of Greek life. She plays a part in many of the most important myths, including the story of the Olympian succession and the Trojan War. Her role as the patron of heroes, including Herakles, Perseus and Bellerophon, makes her central to numerous hero myths. With her distinctive appearance – armed yet wearing a dress – she remains one of the most intriguing of the gods, who, while the epitome of the strong woman, was the patron of male institutions and friend to patriarchy.

Her connections with political institutions and notable heroes have ensured her continued popularity since antiquity. Myths connected with Athena have provided inspiration for numerous thinkers, artists and poets, notably the intriguing story of her birth out of the father's head. With her curious gendered identity, she has been variously denounced as a servant of patriarchy and hailed as a symbol of female achievement.

Athena explores principal aspects of the goddess as she was wor- shipped and represented in the ancient Greek world while taking account of the postclassical transformation of her image. It also high- lights the impact of academic and 'popular' trends upon the under- standing of the goddess in order to provide an indispensable account of a major ancient deity.

Susan Deacy is Senior Lecturer in Greek History and Literature at Roe- hampton University. Her main research interests are Greek religion, and gender and sexuality. Publications include the co-edited volumes *Rape in Antiquity* (1997), and *Athena in the Classical World* (2001), and the monograph *A Traitor to Her Sex? Athena the Trickster* (forthcoming).

Gods and Heroes of the Ancient World

Series editor Susan Deacy
Roehampton University

Routledge is pleased to present an exciting new series, Gods and Heroes of the Ancient World. These figures from antiquity are embedded in our culture, many functioning as the source of creative inspiration for poets, novelists, artists, composers and filmmakers. Concerned with their multifaceted aspects within the world of ancient paganism and how and why these figures continue to fascinate, the books provide a route into understanding Greek and Roman polytheism in the 21st century.

These concise and comprehensive guides provide a thorough understanding of each figure, offering the latest in critical research from the leading scholars in the field in an accessible and approachable form, making them ideal for undergraduates in Classics and related disciplines.

Each volume includes illustrations, time charts, family trees and maps where appropriate.

Also available:

Zeus
Keith Dowden

Prometheus
Carol Dougherty

Medea
Emma Griffiths

Dionysos
Richard Seaford

Oedipus
Lowell Edmunds

ATHENA

Susan Deacy

Routledge
Taylor & Francis Group

LONDON AND NEW YORK

First published 2008
by Routledge
2 Park Square, Milton Park, Abingdon, Oxfordshire OX14 4RN

Simultaneously published in the USA and Canada
by Routledge
711 Third Avenue, New York, NY 10017

Transferred to Digital Printing 2008

Routledge is an imprint of the Taylor & Francis Group, an informa business

© 2008 Susan Deacy

Typeset in Utopia by
RefineCatch Limited, Bungay, Suffolk

British Library Cataloguing in Publication Data
A catalogue record for this book is available from the British Library

Library of Congress Cataloging in Publication Data
Deacy, Susan.
    Athena / Susan Deacy.
        p. cm.
    Includes bibliographical references and index.
    1. Athena (Greek deity).   I. Title.
    BL820.M6D43 2008
    292.2′114—dc22
    2007031417

ISBN13: 978–0–415–30065–0 (hbk)
ISBN13: 978–0–415–30066–7 (pbk)
ISBN13: 978–0–203–93214–8 (ebk)

For Rohan, Jackson and Rhianwen

CONTENTS

SERIES FOREWORD

It is proper for a person who is beginning any serious discourse and task to begin first with the gods.

(Demosthenes, *Epistula* 1.1)

WHY GODS AND HEROES?

The gods and heroes of classical antiquity are part of our culture. Many function as sources of creative inspiration for poets, novelists, artists, composers, filmmakers and designers. Greek tragedy's enduring appeal has ensured an ongoing familiarity with its protagonists' experiences and sufferings, while the choice of Minerva as the logo of one the newest British universities, the University of Lincoln, demonstrates the ancient gods' continued emblematic potential. Even the world of management has used them as representatives of different styles: Zeus and the 'club' culture for example, and Apollo and the 'role' culture: see C. Handy, *The Gods of Management: Who they are, how they work and why they fail*, London, 1978.

This series is concerned with how and why these figures continue to fascinate and intrigue. But it has another aim too, namely to explore their strangeness. The familiarity of the gods and heroes risks obscuring a vital difference between modern meanings and ancient functions and purpose. With certain exceptions, people today do not worship them, yet to the Greeks and Romans they were real beings in a system comprising literally hundreds of divine powers. These ranged from the major gods, each of whom was worshipped in many guises via their epithets or 'surnames', to the heroes – deceased individuals associated with local communities – to other figures such as daimons and nymphs. The landscape was dotted with sanctuaries, while natural features such as mountains, trees and rivers were thought to be inhabited by religious beings. Studying ancient paganism involves finding strategies to comprehend a world where everything was, in the often quoted words of Thales, 'full of gods'.

In order to get to grips with this world, it is necessary to set aside our preconceptions of the divine, shaped as they are in large part by Christianised notions of a transcendent, omnipotent God who is morally good. The Greeks and Romans worshipped numerous beings, both male and female, who looked, behaved and suffered like humans, but who, as immortals, were not bound by the human condition. Far from being omnipotent, each had limited powers: even the sovereign, Zeus/Jupiter, shared control of the universe with his brothers Poseidon/Neptune (the sea) and Hades/Pluto (the underworld). Lacking a creed or anything like an organised church, ancient paganism was open to continual reinterpretation, with the result that we should not expect to find figures with a uniform essence. It is common to begin accounts of the pantheon with a list of the major gods and their function(s) (Hephaistos/Vulcan: craft, Aphrodite/Venus: love, and Artemis/Diana: the hunt and so on), but few are this straightforward. Aphrodite, for example, is much more than the goddess of love, vital though that function is. Her epithets include *hetaira* ('courtesan') and *porne* ('prostitute'), but also attest roles as varied as patron of the citizen body (*pandemos*: 'of all the people') and protectress of seafaring (*Euploia, Pontia, Limenia*).

Recognising this diversity, the series consists not of biographies of each god or hero (though such have been attempted in the past), but of investigations into their multifaceted aspects within the complex world of ancient paganism. Its approach has been shaped partly in response to two distinctive patterns in previous research. Until the middle of the twentieth century, scholarship largely took the form of studies of individual gods and heroes. Many works presented a detailed appraisal of such issues as each figure's origins, myth and cult; these include L.R. Farnell's examination of major deities in his *Cults of the Greek States* (five volumes, Oxford, 1896–1909) and A.B. Cook's huge three-volume *Zeus* (Cambridge, 1914–40). Others applied theoretical developments to the study of gods and heroes, notably (and in the closest existing works to a uniform series), K. Kerényi in his investigations of gods as Jungian archetypes, including *Prometheus: Archetypal image of human existence* (English tr. London 1963) and *Dionysos: Archetypal image of the indestructable life* (English tr. London 1976).

In contrast, under the influence of French structuralism, the later part of the century saw a deliberate shift away from research into particular gods and heroes towards an investigation of the system of which they were part. Fuelled by a conviction that the study of isolated gods could not do justice to the dynamics of ancient religion, the pantheon came to be represented as a logical and coherent network in which the various powers were systematically opposed to one another. In a classic study by J.-P. Vernant for example, the Greek concept of space was shown to be consecrated through the opposition between Hestia (goddess of the hearth – fixed space) and Hermes (messenger and traveller god – moveable space: Vernant, *Myth and Thought Among the Greeks* London, 1983, 127–75). The gods as individual entities were far from neglected however, as may be exemplified by the works by Vernant, and his colleague M. Detienne, on particular deities including Artemis, Dionysos and Apollo: see, most recently, Detienne's *Apollon, le couteau en main: une approche expérimentale du polythéisme grec* (Paris, 1998).

In a sense, this series is seeking a middle ground. While approaching its subjects as unique (if diverse) individuals, it pays attention to their significance as powers within the collectivity of religious beings. *Gods and Heroes of the Ancient World* sheds new light on many of the most important religious beings of classical antiquity; it also provides a route into understanding Greek and Roman polytheism in the twenty-first century.

The series is intended to interest the general reader as well as being geared to the needs of students in a wide range of fields from

Greek and Roman religion and mythology, classical literature and anthropology, to Renaissance literature and cultural studies. Each book presents an authoritative, accessible and refreshing account of its subject via three main sections. The introduction brings out what it is about the god or hero that merits particular attention. This is followed by a central section which introduces key themes and ideas, including (to varying degrees) origins, myth, cult, and representations in literature and art. Recognising that the heritage of myth is a crucial factor in its continued appeal, the reception of each figure since antiquity forms the subject of the third part of the book. The volumes include illustrations of each god/hero and where appropriate time charts, family trees and maps. An annotated bibliography synthesises past research and indicates useful follow-up reading.

For convenience, the masculine terms 'gods' and 'heroes' have been selected for the series title, although (and with an apology for the male-dominated language), the choice partly reflects ancient usage in that the Greek *theos* ('god') is used of goddesses too. For convenience and consistency, Greek spellings are used for ancient names, except for famous Latinized exceptions, and BC/AD has been selected rather than BCE/CE.

I am indebted to Catherine Bousfield, the editorial assistant until 2004, who (literally) dreamt up the series and whose thoroughness and motivation brought it close to its launch. The hard work and efficiency of her successor, Matthew Gibbons, has overseen its progress to publication, and the former classics publisher of Routledge, Richard Stoneman, has provided support and expertise throughout. The anonymous readers for each proposal gave frank and helpful advice, while the authors' commitment to advancing scholarship while producing accessible accounts of their designated subjects has made it a pleasure to work with them.

Susan Deacy, Roehampton University, June 2005

ACKNOWLEDGEMENTS

I am grateful to Richard Stoneman, the former Classics editor of Routledge, who approached me to write this book. The first assistant editor dealing with the *Gods and Heroes* series, Catherine Bousfield, was a source of support and encouragement for several years. Her successor, Matt Gibbons, has provided helpful comments in the final stages of writing. The readers of my original proposal made pertinent observations.

My friend and collaborator Alexandra Villing has provided encouragement and stimulation throughout the various stages of planning and writing. I am grateful to the various colleagues and students at Manchester and more recently at Roehampton University for their interest and support.

My family have been a source of support, above all my husband Rich, to whom I am indebted for so much, including intellectual stimulation, reading a draft of the book and looking after our baby while I was in the office writing. It would not be the same book without him.

LIST OF ILLUSTRATIONS

Line drawings are my own, unless otherwise stated.

WHY ATHENA?

INTRODUCING ATHENA

Pallas Athena I begin to sing, the glorious goddess, glaukopis, polymetis, unbending of heart, pure parthenos, saviour of cities, courageous.

Tritogeneia (*Homeric Hymn* 28.1–4)

It is hard, O goddess, for a mortal man to know you on meeting you, even one who is very knowing, for you liken yourself to everything.

(Homer, *Odyssey* 13.312–13)

WHO WAS ATHENA?

When Athena is envisaged today it is frequently as the warrior female, a symbol of qualities such as justice, wisdom and the arts. She is also regarded as an image of nationhood thanks to her role as protectress of ancient cities, above all Athens, where her temple the Parthenon remains the city's most distinctive landmark. Her image endures in representations of armed females: the likes of Britannia, the Statue of Liberty, and Justice, a statue of whom towers above the Old Bailey, the Central Criminal Court of England. Representations of the goddess herself are found in many Western cities including my own city, Cardiff, where a bust by William Taylor from 1896 stands on top of a nineteenth-century building in the Hayes. This building was originally a public library, so what the artist was drawing on was her association with learning. Now, incidentally, it is an arts centre, in which role it continues to be appropriate as a building with an Athena connection.

The goddess as she is perceived today is an intriguing topic. Our major concern in this book, however, is with the goddess as she was perceived and worshipped by the ancient Greeks. When we turn to this topic, we encounter particular issues, two of which I shall outline here because they demonstrate the extent of the challenges ahead:

- For us, Athena's power is predominantly as a symbol. She is not normally worshipped today and when she is, by modern pagans, it will be by minority groups. In antiquity, in contrast, she was one of the major deities in a religion that was embedded in the lives of every individual. Athena's continued familiarity can obscure differences between 'now' and 'then': between what she is for us as an image, and what she meant to those who thought of her as a real being capable of intervening in the lives of mortals.
- The ancient Athena was a strikingly individualised deity, with particular roles and a distinctive appearance that made her in some respects the most powerful anthropomorphic creation of the Greeks. But she was also one god among many in a religious system that is hard for us to confront. We are likely to be used to notions of the divine shaped by Judeo-Christian notions of God as the Supreme Being. Yet even Zeus, the sovereign deity of the Greek pantheon, was limited in his powers. How are we to make sense of a deity like Athena who was one of literally hundreds of divine beings?

To understand the meanings that Athena held for the Greeks, we need to find ways to de-familiarise her. Our own notions about her need to be set aside, as do those that we hold about belief and worship in general. This introduction will set out some of the challenges faced in dealing with Athena and the strategies for meeting these challenges. It will explain the kind of book that this will be, as well as the book it will not be. It will identify some of the most important aspects of her ancient image as a route into understanding what the Greeks regarded as her particular brand of divinity.

CONFRONTING DIVERSITY

The major gods had numerous roles, so that modern conceptualisations of them (Aphrodite as goddess of love, Poseidon as god of the sea, etc.) tend to be over-simple. Athena was especially characterised for her diversity, as I will try to convey by running though some of her manifestations.

A convenient place to start is epithets, which for Athena, as for any deity, point to distinctive aspects of her nature and functions. As Polias, for example, she was evoked as city protectress and as Promachos as 'fighter in front' or 'champion'. Athena Parthenos was Athena 'the maiden'. Athena Hygieia promoted good health, while Athena Nike was a goddess of victory. The longer of the two *Homeric Hymns* to Athena (*Hymn* 28) is handy as a source for understanding the particular role of epithets in her construction. In a limited space, the poet needed to convey her salient qualities. She is, for him, the 'glorious goddess, glaukopis [essentially "gleaming-eyed"], polymetis [sometimes translated "very cunning" but denoting something more like "cunning in many ways"]'. She is also, the list continues, 'unbending of heart, pure parthenos, saviour of cities, courageous, Tritogeneia [probably "Triton-born"]'. Daring, implacable, virgin, cunning practitioner . . . this book will consider why the Greeks worshipped a goddess with so many manifestations. Who was Athena, we will consider: a unified being with numerous specialised qualities? Or is her diversity the point of her nature?

This diversity is also seen in her modes of operation. The gods of the Greeks were multifaceted powers, but Athena was especially so. She was the city protectress for instance, of Athens and of numerous poleis throughout the Greek world. Her roles covered aspects of male existence, not least warfare and skilled activities such as metalwork and horsemanship, but also the patronage of women's work. She was even, as we shall see, linked with childbirth, although only in certain exceptional circumstances. Other fields of activity included health, music, especially the making and playing of the aulos and various activities connected with the sea including navigation and shipbuilding. As the patron of heroes she supported Jason, Odysseus, Herakles, Perseus and Bellerophon to name but a few.

Athena's multifaceted nature makes it hard for us to make definitive statements about her. She was, for instance, a goddess of war, but also a goddess of women's work. She was the virgin goddess, but also a maternal figure in some contexts. When we look at her interaction with other gods, her versatility becomes further apparent. As a power of technology she had affinities with her fellow craft deity Hephaistos. As a power of war, she complemented Ares. She supported Zeus, meanwhile, in his role as guarantor of divine and human justice. There was also something versatile about her in her very nature. As the virgin warrior, for example, she is on one level the opposite of Aphrodite, the power of sexuality and love. But in certain contexts, as we will see, she possesses traits characteristic of that goddess.

Athena is a slippery figure, who eludes straightforward characterisation. Perhaps if we are to seek a clue to understanding her it should be in her connection with metis, with 'cunning'. As polymetis, she was after all, the goddess 'cunning in many ways'. If we seek to make definitive statements concerning her, this is to miss the point. Figures who exhibit metis in Greek myth are typically situation inverters. They frequently manifest themselves as shape shifters, often employing trickery or disguise (cf. Detienne and Vernant 1978). We might take a lesson from what Odysseus says when the goddess reveals her identity to him in Homer, *Odyssey* 13. Odysseus is the mortal from Greek myth who comes closest to Athena as a practitioner of metis. The *polytropos* – 'much-travelled', or 'many-turning' – hero, he even shares Athena's epithet polymetis. With the goddess before him, however, what he draws attention to is her elusiveness. 'It is hard, O goddess', he comments, 'for a mortal man to know you on meeting you', even, he adds, 'one who is very knowing, for you liken yourself to everything' (*Odyssey*: 13 312–13).

If we are to identify any quality of Athena, then, that underlies a number of her modes of operation, it should be her cunning. But rather than enabling us to sum her up, it shows us that the point of Athena was that she was ever 'on the move'.

ATHENA AND HER ATTRIBUTES

Athena's multifaceted aspects may be discerned further in her numerous attributes. She is typically depicted as a warrior, helmeted and carrying a shield and spear. Usually, she is shown wearing the aegis as a kind of over-garment: a scaly, serpent-fringed object that enabled her to cause terror or disarm her opponents. This dimension to her power could be enhanced through the frequent inclusion on the aegis of the gorgoneion, which intrigued Freud among others as the epitome of emasculating terror. She had strong connections too with nature thanks to her various animal attributes, including the crow, the sphinx, the serpent and above all the owl, which was so closely connected with Athena that it might be described as her pet or even her familiar.

The range of attributes that attached themselves to Athena is seen to an almost absurd degree in the greatest of ancient representations of her, Pheidias' colossal chryselephantine statue (figure 15) constructed for the inside of the Parthenon. In this representation, the goddess was replete with helmet, shield, spear, aegis and gorgoneion. The helmet itself included a sphinx and a pair of griffins. She was holding a figure of Nike, while a serpent was coiled inside the shield.

Each of her attributes reveals something distinctive about her: her shield and helmet mark her out as a warrior for instance, while the aegis attests her magical, dazzling power. When her attributes are compared with those of other gods, something else emerges about Athena, which enables us to recognise what the Greeks saw as her particular brand of deity. No other god has as many attributes as she does. The thunderbolt, sceptre or eagle, for example, may denote Zeus in vase painting or sculpture, while the trident would be adequate to identify Poseidon. The unusual nature of Athena comes even more to the fore when we consider that many of her fellow goddesses lack distinguishing attributes. One of the vases we will look at in Chapter 1 (figure 2) shows a miniature Athena being born, decked out in her warrior paraphernalia and even wearing a tiny gorgoneion. Among the deities observing her birth, one is possibly Hera, but it is only the fact that she is wearing a crown that leads to this identification. Often, Hera lacks distinctive attributes (Carpenter 1991: 40) as does Aphrodite, to take another example, who is characteristically shown holding a flower or a mirror, neither of which distinguish her in themselves from other females.

Attributes enabled the Greeks to articulate the distinctive features of their gods. They provided a means of expressing their powers in ways communicable to humans. Comparing Athena's attributes to those of her fellow gods provides a route into understanding how she was constructed as a divine being: masculinised but with something curious about this masculinisation.

Why Athena then? She is a vividly individualised deity with a distinctive appearance and characteristic attributes, yet she is difficult to pin down, eluding as she does straightforward characterisation. She was a being diverse even for a deity in ancient polytheism.

THE SCOPE OF THIS BOOK

Structuring this book has been a frustrating process. Various draft outlines were produced before deciding upon the best way to present Athena in all her diversity in around 50,000 words. I offer here my rationale behind the structure of final order the volume has taken.

The starting point will be Athena's birth, not from any desire to write a biography of the goddess: this would be a risky undertaking to say the least, not to mention one that would be methodologically problematic. Ancient gods did not have a single 'life'. There was no single, canonical way of representing them and no 'official' version of their myth. The reason for beginning with Athena's birth is in part one of convenience in that it enables us to confront at the outset some of her most salient and recurrent characteristics. As we shall see, her birth established her as the being with an exceptionally close relationship with Zeus. It also presented her warrior characteristics, born as she was thought to be in a dazzling display of warrior magic so powerful that it led to a temporary suspension of cosmic order. The myth also provided a means of reflecting upon Athena's gendered characteristics, with her birth out of Zeus's head providing an image of the triumph of patriarchy, following, as it does, Zeus's suppression of Athena's mother, Metis.

Where does Greek religion begin? Evidence for early practices and traditions is limited and frustrating and there is a current tendency in scholarship to take the eighth century BC as the starting point for a discussion. All the same, there has long been an interest in Athena's origins and early development. For many, the quest for her origins has provided some sort of key to unlocking her identity and much attention has been devoted to which came first, her feminine traits or her warrior masculinity. Chapter 2 will survey various attempts to explain her early 'history'. Many of the earlier approaches are now seen as outmoded; however, they have shaped much of our modern understandings of Athena. What is more, the work by J.J. Bachofen in the nineteenth century and Jane Harrison and others in the first half of the twentieth century has been drawn on in recent decades in the 'Goddess Movement', whose adherents regard Athena as an amalgam of a prehistoric ancient nature goddess and a later warrior deity. This approach to the goddess will be shown to have flaws but it has been selected as the subject for a chapter because of its impact upon modern thinking about the goddess.

Writing this book entails something of a compromise: striking a balance between providing an authoritative account that covers Athena's key roles and qualities on the one hand while striving to capture what it was about the goddess that made her so appealing to the ancients. A study of Athena produced in an earlier generation of scholarship would in likelihood, in the tradition of Farnell (1896–1909) and Cook (1914–40), have identified her various epithets and attributes, examined her sanctuaries and festivals, and explored how vase painters and sculptors sought to depict her image. The benefits of such an approach would be that it ought to avoid omitting anything significant as regards ways of worshipping and representing Athena. Farnell's five-volume *Cults of the Greek*

States is a masterly work, still useful as a source of information of Athena and each of the other gods it covers. For an account of many aspects of Zeus, Cook's three-volume, five-part study remains unrivalled. The problem with such approaches is that they are unlikely to recover what it was that distinguished Athena (or any other being) as a deity, what the relationship was between her various roles and manifestations and whether there was any logic linking her various aspects. What is more, such approaches overlook an integral element in Greek religion, the belief in a pantheon of divine beings. Adopting a 'god by god' approach risks providing a false sense of deities as isolated beings rather than as part of a network of gods.

Chapter 3 will deal with a possible route into understanding both Athena's particular brand of divinity and her place within the pantheon. In the wake of the structuralist-influenced 'Paris School' methodology of Jean-Pierre Vernant, Marcel Detienne and others, it has become practically impossible to discuss Greek gods without reference to the polytheistic system of which they were part, even if like Walter Burkert (1985: 217–18), one is sceptical of their approach. The pantheon emerges in this work as a logical system: a network of interrelating beings each of whom has a coherent place within that system. We will explore the applicability of structuralism as a vehicle for shedding light upon Athena's interactions with other gods. The approach will be tested as a route into understanding Athena via three case studies: of Athena's relationship with Poseidon in relation to the horse and the sea, of her interactions with Hephaistos as a god of craft, and of her connections with her fellow warrior, Ares. Our focus will be on Athena's metis or 'cunning', as it is this quality that has become the standard way to understand her various fields of operation and to explain how it is that she is distinguished from other deities. As well as looking at how the approach can elucidate Athena, using this methodology can also shed light on how polytheistic religion worked. Athena might be seen as a kind of glue that played a role in holding the system together: a unifying factor that helped prevent it being a random agglomeration of gods.

The next chapter will explore one of Athena's most important ancient roles, that of the patron of heroes. We will examine the help she gives to a range of heroes, including those on quests like Perseus and Herakles, and warriors like Achilleus and Diomedes. The divine qualities that are brought to bear in her interventions in the lives of these individuals will be explored, above all her metis. We will see that, as well as being a dedicated friend, she was a dangerous enemy as well. A guiding principle behind her interventions on behalf of Achilleus, Herakles et al. was the notion of 'helping friends, harming enemies', a central tenet of the Greek morality. We will explore the applicability of the 'helping friends, harming enemies' maxim by looking at those who suffer at her hands, especially the Trojans, who moved from being one of her favoured peoples to her enemies.

From the earliest times, Athena was intimately associated with Athens, with her very name connected with the name of the city. As well as the city's patron, she was connected with its identity so that, as Athens developed into a powerful and prosperous city, the image of Athena thrived. Substantially more evidence exists for Athens than for any other city, enabling us to chart in some detail her cult, temples and festivals and her role in local myths. Our first chapter focusing on Athens, Chapter 5, will examine the qualities of Athena that enabled her to be venerated above other deities. The focus will be on her relationships with other important Attic gods, including Zeus, Poseidon and Hephaistos. There will be a detailed examination of her role in Athenian foundation myths, particularly the story of the birth of Erichthonios, Athena's protégé and even, in an important sense, her 'son'.

Greek religion was in many respects a conservative religion, with particular beliefs and practices remaining intact over centuries. Conversely, it was a notoriously open system, susceptible to change in response to developing conditions and to the varying needs of its worshippers. Our discussion of Athena in Athens will be organised largely in accordance with this duality. After the mostly thematic account of Chapter 5, we will trace the development of her cult from the earliest times down to the sixth and fifth centuries when Athena came to hold a particular appeal as city patron, embodying the city's aspirations and even its self image. These centuries saw rich representations in public art and on vases matched with a prominent role in literature and myth. Certain of her cults and

festivals were embellished, notably the Panathenaia which continued to be aggrandized as the city grew.

Chapter 6 will examine early developments in Athena's cult. It
will consider how far back the cult can be traced though a study
of the possible Mycenaean veneration of Athena. From this it will
look at the effect of the synoecism or unification of Attica upon the
meaning of the goddess for the Athenians, whereby Athena's cult
became the major cult of the whole state, giving Athena a centrality
unique in the Greek world. Evidence for Athena becomes more
plentiful in the sixth century, particularly around the time of the
Peisistratid tyranny, under which Athena was celebrated as the
patron goddess of the newly prosperous city. Athena's popularity
continued into the early fifth century as we will see by looking at
events of the Persian Wars, including the invasion of the city in 480
when the sack of the city under Athena's protection failed to
dampen the people's reverence for their goddess.

While Chapter 6 surveys developments over several centuries,
Chapter 7 focuses upon the second half of the fifth century BC,
when, with Athens at the peak of its power and prosperity, there
came to be a closer than ever identification between goddess and
polis. We will examine this extraordinary period for Athenian history
and for the role of Athena, which, though short-lived, has produced
some of the most enduring images of the goddess.

As Chapter 8 will show, there was far more to Athena than the
Athenian goddess. She was worshipped widely throughout the
Greek world, throughout the mainland and the islands, as well as in
the more peripheral areas of Greek influence. In each locality, distinctive ways were found to worship her, with particular festivals,
epithets and myths. She was regularly, as at Athens, venerated as
the armed protectress, although a range of other qualities are also
apparent, including some intriguing 'fertility'-like traits. The examination of the wider Greek world will enable us to explore the
diversity of Athena throughout Greece. It will also contextualise the
Athenian evidence, by elucidating how far Athens was distinctive
among the poleis in its depiction of the goddess.

All the books in this series concern figures who have had, to
varying degrees, a place in the postclassical world, so that, after they

stopped being worshipped, they were adopted for their symbolic appeal. My last chapter will consider how the goddess we are familiar with today emerged out of the deity worshipped by the Greeks. It will explore the uses made of Athena's image by the early Christians and, above all, the postclassical world. Originally reviled as a pagan deity, her image was ultimately regarded as conducive to Christianised virtues including Justice and, above all, Wisdom, with her image utilised by various regimes, from monarchies to revolutionary France.

The final section of the chapter will present a striking instance of Athena's diversity as an image by looking at feminist uses of the goddess, which have variously celebrated her as an image of powerful femininity and depicted her as a patriarchal 'sell out'. On the one hand, a variety of 'Athena projects' have been formed in recent decades, where the goddess serves as a kind of figurehead for educational organisations that serve to promote women and girls' involvement in such fields as science, mathematics and technology. While these projects seek to find a place for females within traditionally male-dominated fields, the other tendency has been to regard Athena as a traitor to her sex who sides with the male at the expense of other females. Feminist theory has presented Athena as the archetype of the strong female who, far from paving the way for other women to succeed, ensures that she remains the exception. This has given a mythic dimension to what women dominant in public and political life have been accused of throughout history, most strikingly of all in recent years: Margaret Thatcher.

We will deal with the rationale behind these and other trends in the reception of Athena, while exploring the relationship between modern manifestations and the ancient deity. As her ancient image is a diverse one, we will consider which aspects have been drawn on, and which ones, less conducive to postclassicism, have been omitted. This will enable reflection on how far 'our' Athena is rooted in classical ideas, and how far she is the product of her postclassical reception.

To keep discussion focused, I have chosen not to include endnotes. Key references are provided in the main text. Items for further reading are provided in the 'Further Reading' section.

NOTE ON SPELLING AND TRANSLATIONS

There was more than one name for the goddess in the Greek world. In epic she was Athenaiē, contracted to Athene. The Doric form was Athana and in Aeolic Greek she was Athanaa. The Attic form of her name, Athenaia was contracted to Athena, the form that came to be dominant from the fourth century. For personal preference I have opted for the Attic 'Athena' instead of the common alternative 'Athene'.

I have opted, where practicable for Hellenised spelling (e.g. Peisistratos rather than Pisistratus). To reflect its cultic and cultural importance, the Athenian Akropolis is spelt with an upper case 'A'.

The translations in this book are my own unless otherwise stated.

KEY THEMES

THE BIRTH OF ATHENA

Nobody is the mother that gave birth to me, and I approve of the male in every respect, with all my heart, with the exception of undergoing marriage, and I am exceedingly of the father.

(Aeschylus, *Eumenides*: 736–8)

INTRODUCTION: HARDLY A HEADACHE

The birth of Athena is typically recounted today as a story with humorous potential: Zeus has a 'splitting' headache, Hephaistos takes out his axe to relieve the pain, and out comes Athena. That such an interpretation was possible in antiquity is evident from one of Lucian's second-century AD *Dialogues of the Gods*. 'What's this? A girl in armour?' is what Hephaistos exclaims as he sees the result of his actions, 'she's got *glaukos* ('fierce') eyes, but they go very well with her helmet'. But the majority of the sources present Athena's birth in less frivolous terms, as a story with strong aetiological ('explanatory') components. As this chapter will consider, it explained key things about Athena including how she came to be born, what her relationship was to her father, and how she acquired certain of her characteristics and attributes. It also dealt with larger events concerning the development of the Olympian pantheon and Zeus's emergence as the sovereign power in the universe.

The interpretation of any Greek deity is aided by an awareness of their perceived origins, but to come in any way close to an understanding of Athena, it is necessary to examine the story of her birth. But what exactly was the myth? In a culture that lacked any single, canonical version of stories, it was continually open to adaptation and transformation. Such was its popularity that in some circumstances it only needed to be alluded to rather than narrated at length as is the case even in the earliest references to the story, those in the Homeric epics, where Athena is described as *Dios ekgegauia* ('Zeus-born': e.g. *Odyssey*: 6.229) and where her birth was already the cause of a special intimacy between father and daughter. At one point in the *Iliad*, Ares complains to Zeus about the favouritism shown to Athena at his own expense, the reason given being *autos egeinao* ('you fathered her' or, more likely, 'you gave birth to her': 5.880). In the brief sketch that follows, I am making no attempt to provide some all-encompassing, archetypal form of the myth, but rather am aiming to indicate recurrent trends in order to introduce some of the aspects that we will be discussing.

- Zeus received a prophecy that the second child born to his wife, the Titaness Metis, would overthrow him as he had overthrown his father Kronos, and Kronos had before that overthrown his own father Ouranos.
- Metis was a type of Greek deity who was able to shape shift; when she was pregnant with her first child, Athena, Zeus tricked her into turning herself into something tiny, and then swallowed her.
- Athena was released from Zeus's body by the craft god, Hephaistos – or in some accounts Prometheus – by cracking open his head with an axe.
- Athena sprang forth, sometimes fully grown, but in any case in full armour, brandishing her weapons and crying: not the cry of a newborn baby but that of a warrior.
- The gods looked on startled, and the whole of the universe was thrown into disarray by the noise and the spectacle. As for Hephaistos, he is typically depicted fleeing from the scene with his axe.
- Having emerged, Athena removed her weapons and the universe returned to normal.

- The site of her birth was usually a river called Triton, variously situated in Libya and certain Greek locations including sites in Arcadia, Boiotia and Krete.

After a brief survey of possible Near Eastern antecedents, we will introduce some of the salient aspects of the myth via a look at two visual representations and then a literary account, the longer of the two Homeric Hymns to Athena. After that, we will explore its place within the Olympian succession myth. Finally we will consider the gendered aspects to the story and their implications for understanding Athena's character and functions.

ANTECEDENTS

Among the numerous approaches that have been developed for the study of Greek myth, two in particular have had a bearing upon how to tackle the story of Athena's birth. Fuelled by the 'Paris School' of Vernant, Detienne and others (Chapter 3), there has been a strong focus since the mid-twentieth century on the implications of particular stories for shaping our understanding of the beliefs and values of the people that possessed and transmitted them irrespective of the origins and early development of the stories in question. On the other hand, recent years have seen a renewed interest in the early development of the myths, particularly via a consideration of their eastern heritage. This section will survey some of the attempts that have been made to determine the oriental motifs and traditions behind the story of Athena's birth while assessing whether the quest has any bearing on our interpretation of the Greek versions of the myth.

The early archaic period saw what has been described as an 'orientalising revolution' with the Near East exerting a profound influence upon Greek culture, the development of the alphabet being one facet of this as well as developments in art and mythology. Parallels have been discerned between Greek myths and the much older Near Eastern material including the Hittite myth known as the *Kingdom in Heaven*, which has been hailed as the inspiration for the Hesiodic account of the divine succession (see below). In order to overthrow the heaven god, Anu, Kumarbi bit off and swallowed his genitals. Discovering that this act had impregnated him, he spat out the semen but the weather god Teššub remained inside and needed to be cut out of him, as it seems did other deities including one called ᵈKA.ZAL, who possibly emerged out of his skull (West 1999: 278–9; 280). The text is too fragmentary to enable us to do anything more than speculate as to whether ᵈKA.ZAL's birth lies behind the story of Athena's head birth but it at least raises the possibility of a Hittite background to the story.

Moving to Mesopotamian myth, a more promising antecedent may be discerned: the story of the ascent from the netherworld of Inanna, the principal goddess of the Mesopotamian pantheon, a deity similar to Athena in certain regards as a warrior (though also the love goddess) whose attributes included the owl. Trapped in the netherworld, Inanna had lost the seven garments that represented her holy power or *me* but on her return, she emerged fully clothed once more, reborn resplendent in her power, the spectacle of the emerging goddess causing her fellow god Dumezi to flee the scene. In the story of Inanna's return, we may have the origins of Athena's emergence, decked out in the attributes that represent her power. To add to the possibility, both stories involve an intermediary, the craft gods Enki and Hephaistos, who enable the goddess in question to be released. Enki, the god of wisdom and craft, the keeper of the *me*, created two figures, kur-gar-ra and gala-tur-ra who, on his instructions, sprinkled her body with the food and water of life.

The possibility that this story was an inspiration for Athena's birth looks more appealing still when we take account of its possible mountain symbolism. In his investigation of parallels with Mesopotamian myth, Charles Penglase (1994: 232–3) draws attention to some of the words used for Zeus's head, among them *to karēnon* which can also denote a mountain peak and *koryphē*, the crown of the head or the peak of a mountain. Depictions of Inanna's return in Mesopotamian art, meanwhile, show her standing on a mountain representing the netherworld.

It should be stressed, however, that finding antecedents can only go part of the way to explaining the reasons for a myth. If the motif does have its origins in the Near East, it has been transformed in a distinctively Greek context to depict the particular features of Athena, the warrior with an exceptionally close relationship with her father. In what follows the emphasis will shift from the question of where the story came from to the uses made of it by the Greeks.

CAPTURING THE MOMENT

Visual representations serve as a convenient starting point for our analysis because of the nature of the medium. Artists needed to make their subjects immediately recognisable by conveying, as succinctly as possible, key features of the story. In the two vases that we will examine in this section, each artist has selected the moment that is the common feature of visual representations of the birth: Athena's emergence out of the head of Zeus. There are a number of differences between the two depictions, a consideration of which will enable us to demonstrate the versatility of the myth and introduce some of the aspects of the myth we will explore later in this chapter.

In figure 1, an Attic black-figure lip cup from *c.* 560 BC, Athena is emerging out of Zeus's head while the 'midwife', Hephaistos, is fleeing the scene. The reason for the choice of only three participants is in part consistency with the other side of the vase on which Athena and Zeus are again present, again with a third figure, this time Herakles (see figure 4). In addition, it would presumably have been in the artist's interests to make the scene as simple as possible because the image on the cup is only a tiny one, of about 3cm × 2cm. In his little painting, the artist has managed to pack in a great many details, expressing the relationship between the three figures and their reaction to the events. In among the most striking depictions of father–daughter closeness, Athena is holding her spear aloft in a gesture that parallels that of Zeus as he wields the thunderbolt so that, even as she is being born, Athena is seen to act in partnership with her father. At the same time, she has not yet fully emerged, a detail which effectively makes her an attribute of Zeus, as yet not fully separated from her father.

Figure 1 Athena emerging from the head of Zeus while Hephaistos flees the scene, Attic black-figure cup, London, British Museum B 424.

As for the third figure, Hephaistos, he is fleeing from the scene carrying the axe that broke open Zeus's head, a detail that brings out something lacking in literary accounts, namely the apparent hostility towards him on the part of Zeus and Athena, both of whom are brandishing a weapon in his direction. This makes him, effectively, the first joint enemy that they need to face. Rather than seeking to relieve Zeus of his headache, we seem to be being presented with a less well-intentioned attempt to wound Zeus. Hephaistos is here more like Prometheus, who in some sources is said to have delivered the violent blow and whose inimical relationship to Zeus is a recurrent feature of Greek myth (see Dougherty 2005: esp. 31–4, 71–2). As this chapter unfolds I will consider some possible reasons for Hephaistos' actions, and in Chapter 3, further possibilities will be proposed when we come to explore Athena's relationship with the craft god. In the meantime, suffice it to say that this vase presents us with a range of features, notably the closeness of Athena and Zeus who act in concert against Hephaistos even as the goddess is being born.

More elaborate is figure 2, an Attic black-figure amphora from around 540, which, being so much larger, is able to include many more details. Hephaistos is not present this time. Eileithyia, the birth attendant goddess, has the more customary role of midwife while another female and two males are observing Athena's emergence. Athena is clothed once again in a dress but also a helmet, which is merging into the decorative pattern at the top of the vase, a shield and a spear. Over her dress, she wears another of her attributes, the aegis, which contains a little rectangular gorgoneion. Athena is not 'supposed' to be wearing the aegis at this stage, because according to literary accounts, it is something that she acquires subsequently – either as something given to her by Hephaistos, or as an object that she herself fashions out of the flayed skin of a defeated enemy (e.g. Apollodoros 1.6.2: the giant Pallas; Cicero, *De Natura Deorum* 3.23.59; Clement of Alexandria, *Exhortation to the Greeks* 2.28: a father called Pallas). Similarly, the head of the Gorgon is given to her in myth by Perseus after he beheads the monster with her assistance (Chapter 4). Vase paintings, however, are not meant to be chronologically accurate: the artist is showing the consummate goddess, small-scale though fully formed, decked out in her warrior paraphernalia.

An especially striking feature of the scene is the frontal depiction of the two central figures. Figures in Greek art are usually depicted in profile with frontality reserved for those who are monstrous, or in some other respect out of the ordinary, dangerous and ambiguous. Dionysos, the god of excess, drunkenness and abandon is at times depicted thus, as are people who have died or who are on the verge of death. Frontally depicted figures are those who upset norms, which is why frontality is a trait of the Gorgon, whose peculiar blend of animal and human traits, as well as male and female ones, marks her out as the most ugly and dangerous of all monsters. This frontal depiction of Zeus and Athena is a means, perhaps, of emphasising that something strange and extraordinary is taking place, something that confounds the usual state of things. As on the cup, Zeus is holding his distinctive attribute, the thunderbolt, but it serves a very

Figure 2 The birth of Athena in the presence of several deities, Attic black-figure amphora, Virginia Museum of Fine Arts, Richmond 60.23. The Arthur and Margaret Glasgow Fund. Photo: Katherine Wetzel. © Virginia Museum of Fine Arts.

different purpose. Far from wielding it as a defensive weapon, he is grasping it between his hands, as a means, perhaps, of dealing with the pain of childbirth. What the artist seems to be indicating is that, in appropriating the female ability to give birth, he suffers the pain associated with it too. There is a nice gender inversion here: the king of the gods has taken on the role that is quintessentially female, while Athena emerges in full armour.

The attributes of the two male witnesses, a kerykion (herald's staff) and armour, show them to be, respectively, the messenger god Hermes and Ares, the male power of war, who offsets Athena the female warrior. Eileithyia is shown to our left. We would expect the female on the other side to be a second Eileithyia, except that she is wearing a crown, a detail that makes it likely that she is Hera, Zeus's wife. Her body language, with one fist clenched, may well be expressing her displeasure at what has taken place; after all, she typically reacts adversely to her husband's production of children outside their marriage, notably Herakles (Chapter 4), also Apollo and in some accounts Athena. In the *Homeric Hymn to Pythian Apollo*, for example, Hera accuses Zeus of giving birth to 'Glaukopis Athena who is foremost among all the blessed gods' (314–15) as a deliberate attempt to surpass her parthenogenic ('without fertilisation by a male') production of Hephaistos who was 'shrivelled of foot, a shame to me and weakly' (316–17). This points us towards why Hephaistos may be absent from the scene, namely because Hera is there instead as the one with the ambivalent reaction, rather than her son. Although the details are different, a thematic consistency is apparent in that, in each case, Athena's emergence impacts upon the society of the gods, here causing Hera's displeasure, and elsewhere leading Athena and Zeus to wield their weapons towards Hephaistos. We will turn now to a poetic account of the myth and its effects upon those who witnessed it.

COSMIC TERROR: THE HOMERIC HYMN TO ATHENA

In *Homeric Hymn* 28 *To Athena*, the radiant spectacle of the emerging goddess throws the whole universe into disarray:

> Metieta Zeus himself gave birth to her out of his terrible head, arrayed in warlike arms, golden, gleaming. Astonishment seized the gods as they watched. She sprang forth at once from the immortal head and stood before Zeus who holds the aegis, shaking a sharp spear. Great Olympos began to quake dreadfully at the might of Glaukopis, and earth all about screamed horribly, and the sea moved and frothed with dark waves, while foam suddenly burst forth. The brilliant son of Hyperion stopped his swift-footed horses for a long time, until the girl, Pallas Athena, stripped the godlike armour from her immortal shoulders, and Metieta Zeus rejoiced.
>
> (*Homeric Hymn* 28.5–16)

As she breaks forth out of Zeus's head, her 'golden, gleaming' weapons present a dazzling spectacle, while her eyes too blaze forth light. Athena is Glaukopis, a title that is often translated as 'grey-eyed', with other possibilities being 'blue-eyed' or 'green-eyed', but it is lightness or brightness that is the key rather than any particular hue. A more apt translation is 'gleaming-eyed' or 'darting-eyed', or even 'owl-eyed', from the glaux, the little owl, which with its big eyes, night vision and tendency to make sudden appearances was a fitting attribute of the goddess (see figure 3 below). This is the same dazzling brightness that is a feature of other epiphanies including Athena's sudden appearance before Achilleus in the *Iliad* when he was on the verge of killing Agamemnon and 'terribly did her eyes flash' (1.200). This tendency is present even in the Lucian dialogue discussed at the start of this chapter where I opted for the translation 'fierce' to capture the contrast between the attractiveness, for Hephaistos, of the emerging goddess and the spectacle of her *glaukos* stare.

The gods look on in amazement as Athena leaps forth, while heaven 'quaked dreadfully', earth 'screamed horribly', the sea 'moved and frothed with dark waves', and the sun ('the brilliant son of Hyperion') stopped his passage across the sky. Athena – gleaming, dazzling, golden as she is – has temporarily taken over the sun's role. Her birth is similar to a degree with the birth of another golden child of Zeus, Apollo:

> So she [Leto] cast her arms about a palm tree and kneeled on the soft meadow while the earth laughed for joy beneath. Then the child leaped forth to the light,

and all the goddesses raised a cry. Straightaway, great Phoibos, the goddesses washed you purely and cleanly with sweet water, and swathed you in a white garment of fine texture, new-woven, and fastened a golden band about you.

(*Hymn to Delian Apollo* 117–22, Loeb translation, slightly adapted)

With a bright name – Phoibos or 'Shining One' – and bright attributes, this is a fitting epiphany of the god associated with the sun. His agile birth, springing forth 'to the light' recalls Athena's emergence from Zeus's head except that while Earth 'laughed for joy' at the prospect of Apollo's birth, the birth of Athena caused an earthquake. The radiant brilliance of Phoibos is to be contrasted to the flashing, terror-inducing epiphany of Glaukopis, that can replace the sun as giver of light. A closer parallel for Athena's dangerous, dazzling brightness is what happens when Zeus uses his power against the Titans:

From Heaven and from Olympos he came immediately, hurling his lightning: the bolts flew thick and fast from his strong hand together with thunder and lightning, whirling an awesome flame. The life-giving earth crashed around in burning, and the vast wood crackled loud with fire all about. All the land seethed, and Ocean's streams and the unfruitful sea. The hot vapour lapped round the earthborn Titans: flame unspeakable rose to the bright upper air: the flashing glare of the thunderstone and lightning blinded their eyes for all that they were strong.

(689–700, Loeb translation, slightly adapted)

As on the occasion of Athena's birth, the whole kosmos is affected with normal order suspended. Perhaps this is what the artist of figure 1 had in mind in showing Zeus wielding the thunderbolt while the emerging Athena is shaking her spear, with the warrior spectacle of her birth comparable to the effects produced by the weapon of Zeus. In the moment she is being born, she is like her father, with power that can dazzle the universe. There is something impetuous about her birth, breaking out as she does from the head of Zeus displaying power that is reminiscent of his own.

The terror exists only, however, until Athena breaks the spell by removing her golden armour. Her war magic is capable of generating cosmic chaos, but she can also turn off her power and restore order and peace. This movement from warmonger to peace-bringer seems to be signalled by the change of names. While emerging in her armour, she is Glaukopis; when she removes the amour she is 'the girl Pallas Athena', the ally of Zeus who ends the cosmic terror. Then, the epiphany over, 'Metieta Zeus rejoiced'. Ultimately, her birth brings pleasure, like Apollo's birth did and the hymn ends by depicting the closeness between Athena and the father who delights in her. As we shall see throughout this book, Athena is a goddess who embodies various contradictions including masculinity/femininity and war/peace. In the hymn, her duality is evident from the moment of her birth. She is the dangerous warrior but also a peace-bringer. She displays an otherness so extreme that it can stop the universe from functioning properly but she is capable of detaching herself from that power and aligning herself with Zeus.

A different perspective can be offered on this duality if we take one step back, to explore the events that led up to her birth. This will necessitate an examination of the myth of the divine succession, the story of how Zeus came first of all to be ruler of the universe and then secured this rule for all time through the birth of Athena. Our discussion will enable us to move to an under-standing of one further aspect of the hymn, Zeus's epithet Metieta, sometimes translated as 'wise' but more specifically denoting something like 'Metis-ized'. When Zeus gives birth to Athena, he does so as one who possesses Metis ('cunning'), the goddess who was pregnant with Athena when, to protect his future, Zeus swallowed her.

THE SUCCESSION MYTH AND THE DEFEAT OF THE MOTHER

Athena's birth is often depicted as something that appears *ex nihilo*, a phenomenon without apparent precedents. In Margaret Atwood's *Lady Oracle* (1976: 258), for example, it is used in relation to the novel's heroine, to denote her sudden appearance on the literary scene as the author of a critically-acclaimed work of poetry. But it also forms part of, and resolves, the story concerning how Zeus came to power: a story that begins in the earliest days of the cosmos. According to the best-known (and earliest) account, in Hesiod's *Theogony*, Gaia (Earth) gave birth through parthenogenesis to Ouranos (Heaven), who became her husband; however, he prevented their children from being born by keeping them imprisoned within their mother. In time, Gaia equipped her youngest son, Kronos, with a sickle, and he used this in order to castrate his father. Kronos married Rhea, and received a prophecy from Gaia and Ouranos that one of his sons would overthrow him. In an attempt to avert the same fate that befell his father, he swallowed his children as soon as they emerged. But when the youngest, Zeus, was born, Rhea gave him a stone to swallow instead, and tricked by his wife, he disgorged each of the children, and Zeus arose as ruler in his father's place.

Zeus should have fallen prey to the same fate as his father and grandfather before him. While his first wife, Metis, was pregnant with Athena, he received a prophecy – again from Gaia and Ouranos – that their second child, a son, would overthrow him. However, he came up with a response that outdid the actions of either of his ancestors. Ouranos stuffed his children back inside their mother, and Kronos ate his children, but what Zeus did was to swallow his wife, 'craftily deceiving her with cunning words' as Hesiod puts it, to 'put her in his own belly, so that the goddess might devise for him both good and evil' (*Theogony* 899–900). Not only does this prevent the successor being born, it also ensures that his wife will not be able to take action against him, in the way that Gaia did against Ouranos, or his own mother Rhea did against Kronos.

It also ensures that Zeus will be able to avert fate. Prophesies usually come true in myth, however much individuals seek to escape them, as Kronos discovered and as did Oedipus. But with 'cunning' literally contained within Zeus so that the god has become, as it were, Metis-ized, this one remains permanently unfulfilled. His rule now secure, he embarks upon a series of unions before marrying Hera. It is once he has entered into this final, lasting union that Athena is born:

> Zeus himself gave birth out of his own head to Gleaming-eyed Tritogeneia, Awful, Rouser of Battle, Raiser of the Noise of War, Unwearying, Mistress, who delights in tumults and wars and battles.
>
> (*Theogony* 924–6)

With Athena's birth, the problem of the succession is resolved once and for all:

Ouranos
↓
Kronos
↓
Zeus
↓
Athena

The scheme ends not with the threatened son, but with the daughter who, warrior and warmonger though she is, will not seek to overthrow her father. Broken too is the chain of female power:

Gaia
↓
Rhea
↓
Metis
↓
Athena

Gaia set in motion the succession myth by giving birth to a fatherless son; Zeus now produces a daughter who is denied a relationship with her mother. One of her epithets is polymetis ('cunning in many ways') and the quality of metis is one of her defining features, which, as we will see in subsequent chapters (esp. 3 and 4), underlies many of her spheres of influence. But there is a difference between the cunning of Metis and that of her daughter. Metis was too dangerous to be permitted an independent existence but polymetis Athena is, as it were, a safe version of her mother, who aligns herself with her father and with the patriarchy over which he reigns. The myth is not just about Athena: it is also about who she is not. She is differentiated from Metis, the embodiment of cunning, and from her nameless brother, the child who would have been 'something else, stronger than the thunderbolt' in the words of a variant of Hesiod's account (Hesiod fr. 343.8).

Athena's birth is the product of a temporary mixing up of gender roles. Zeus becomes feminised, giving birth to a child in lieu of his wife, while, in some versions, Hephaistos takes on the role of midwife. The product is a deity who confounds gendered norms, but who, with the close bond established with her father by her birth, safeguards the patriarchal system that comes into place at the time when she was born. As she is made to say in the *Eumenides*, in the passage quoted at the head of this chapter, she is a motherless goddess whose affiliations are at once with her father Zeus and with 'the male' in general. This makes her, in gendered terms, an anomaly: 'the child of Olympian Zeus' as Apollo states earlier in the *Eumenides*, 'who was not even nursed in the darkness of a womb' who is consequently 'such an offspring to which no goddess could give birth' (663–6). The Greeks were fond of exploring Athena's similarities with other pugnacious females, notably the Amazons, the enemies of patriarchy *par excellence*, whose society was represented as a matriarchy and who, on various occasions in myth, launched invasions of Greece. While the Amazons as a race, and individual women like Klytaimnestra, threaten male domination, however, Athena is consistently the upholder of patriarchy, trusted by her father more than any other deity and even given access to his thunderbolt (Aeschylus, *Eumenides* 827–8; Euripides, *Women of Troy* 78–93). This made her an appealing figure to use as a means of exploring gender norms, as one odd and ambiguous but ultimately aligned with order and patriarchy. This duality of Athena will be a recurrent feature of this book. One of the elements that make Athena so appealing for the Greeks, it has also been seized on by modern commentators as a means of explaining her nature.

OVERVIEW

This multi-layered myth has provided a convenient starting point for this book because it was regarded as integral to Athena's character and many of her divine roles. It enables us to confront from the outset particular aspects of the goddess, including her place in the pantheon, her distinctive mixture of masculinity and femininity, her role as a warrior and the cunning that she inherits from her mother via Metieta Zeus. The myth establishes Athena's close relationship with her father, and with 'the male' in general. A warrior female who ought to be subversive and transgressive, she uses her power in concert with her father from the moment of her birth. More broadly, her birth brings to an end the problem of the succession and underlines Zeus's status as the sovereign power over the universe. A diverse figure, she is at once magical, powerful and dangerous and also the upholder of order.

2

TRACING ATHENA'S ORIGINS

We do not know where the Greek gods came from, but the conventional view is that most of them came from somewhere else.

(Hurwit 1999: 12)

INTRODUCTION: DO ORIGINS MATTER?

One of the current methodological issues in the study of Greek religion is the question of the origins and early development of the gods. Until the second half of the twentieth century, it was commonplace to understand their nature and roles by determining their supposed origins and prehistoric development. With these issues decided upon, it was thought that an understanding of all subsequent manifestations could be reached. Origins, in short, were thought to supply a key to uncovering the nature of individual gods. In contrast, in the wake of the structuralist-influenced work of Vernant, Detienne and others, the emphasis has shifted from origins to what may be termed 'contexts'. It has become customary to look not to the question of prehistoric formation, but to the contexts in which the gods appear in archaic, classical and subsequent representations. To understand Athena, for example, scholars have regularly looked not at where her cult and persona may have originated but at her place in the complex religious system that is the pantheon (Chapter 3).

However, an interest in origins has not gone away. The work by

Walter Burkert, Martin West and others on the impact of Near Eastern influences upon Greek thought has led to a renewed interest in the early development of the gods. Martin Bernal's *Black Athena* project, meanwhile, though encountering criticism from specialists in a range of areas, has re-opened the origins question to a new generation of critics. Moreover, outside the 'academy' various feminist authors, poets and artists maintain an interest in Athena's prehistorical formation, often citing as evidence earlier generations of scholars including J.J. Bachofen and two of the 'greats' of early scholarship on Greek religion, Jane Harrison and M.P. Nilsson.

This chapter will begin by exploring one particularly prevalent route that has been taken in an attempt to explain Athena's origins, namely to seek the alleged point in prehistory when her character came to be determined. This will entail both a survey of early scholarship and of uses of this material in certain feminist circles since the 1970s. As we shall see, the approach has come in for cogent criticism. Because of its place in the history of scholarship on Athena, however, not to mention its ongoing role in shaping how many people perceive Athena, it will be covered in the following sections.

ATHENA, MATRIARCHY AND THE GODDESS MOVEMENT

With her curious blend of gendered traits, the figure of Athena has been an appealing one in the so-called 'goddess movement', whose adherents hold the belief that in prehistory there existed a matriarchy, where women were dominant in society and where religion centred on the worship of a 'Great Goddess', a peaceful, nurturing being whose areas of concern included nature and fertility. This system, it is held, was eventually overthrown in the Bronze Age by the emerging patriarchy, when men seized control of society and imposed the worship of a male-dominated pantheon presided over by the sovereign Zeus. The belief in a matriarchal period has been a major feature of feminist spirituality since the 1970s when, in the wake of the feminist resurgence of that decade, it was embraced as a means of celebrating the religious power considered to be inherent in 'the feminine'. In the quest for a separate feminine identity, this primordial matriarchy has come to be hailed as a 'golden age', a time when human society was guided by the very values advanced as ideals in feminist circles including nurturing and peaceful co-operation among women.

While the theory has been embraced by successions of novelists, poets and artists, it has been viewed sceptically to say the least by many academics, not least through its reliance upon what are seen as outmoded and methodologically non-viable interpretations of archaeological and literary evidence. In seeking some universal 'truth' about prehistory, it has been argued, the Goddess Movement overlooks the diversity of the evidence at our disposal. The approaches diverge to such a degree that in recent decades a rift has emerged between 'feminist spiritualists' on the one hand and on the other hand scholars, generally themselves feminists, who have used their expertise to seek alternative ways of interpreting the evidence. I will set out key aspects of the theory in relation to Athena, while drawing attention to its shortcomings as a means of enlightening either the formation of the goddess or her subsequent manifestations.

Along with various other ancient goddesses from Greece and beyond, Athena has been interpreted as a survival of significantly older beings, themselves survivals of the hypothesised Great Goddess. Her various connections with birds and serpents have been explained as survivals of a bird and snake goddess thought to be worshipped in early human societies. On this interpretation, passages such as Homer, *Odyssey* 3.371–3, where she transforms herself into a vulture, would be viewed as an echo of a time when her original form was ornithological. Such an interpretative model is appealing too in relation to the owl, which is not only her attribute (or even pet) but in places even a possible epiphany of the goddess, as in figure 3, where, on an Attic mug from the second quarter of the fifth century BC, the creature is kitted out in her distinctive apparel.

As for Athena's warrior appearance and attributes, these are regarded as having been acquired at the time of the patriarchal takeover, when the Olympian gods emerged supreme and, it is argued, Athena was adopted by the new system as a warrior deity,

Figure 3 Armed owl, Attic red-figure mug, Paris, Louvre CA 2192; redrawn by S.J. Deacy.

with her original nature concealed behind the persona of the warrior virgin. What we have with this interpretation is a catch-all way of explaining Athena, with both sides of her nature explained by fitting them into either the hypothesised original matriarchy or the more violent, warlike system thought to have overtaken it. This has led to one of the most enduring feminist interpretations of Athena, that of the 'traitor to her sex' who had her origins among the primordial Goddess worshippers but who ended up part of a patriarchal system as kind of proto-Mrs Thatcher who combined her unique powers as a strong female with an affiliation to male concerns and structures. Athena has been regarded as the ultimate sell-out, the female who used her power not to assist other women, but on behalf of males. She has even come in for attack as though she were a real person who deliberately colluded in the alleged patriarchal conquest. Kate Millett, for example, writing towards the start of the feminist 'second wave', envisaged her as the figure who 'marches on, spoiling to betray her kind' (1971: 114). Decades earlier, Jane Harrison lamented the role played by Athena in the rise of patriarchy whereby 'the maiden of the elder stratum' or the 'Lost Leader' (1903: 303) was divested of her femininity. At once a victim who was de-sexed in the transition to patriarchy, she was also, for Harrison, the victimiser who colluded in the suppression of women.

BACHOFEN AND 'MOTHER-RIGHT'

Steeped as it is in the feminist thinking of the 1970s onwards, it might be thought that the theory of an original matriarchy is a relatively recent development, but as we have just seen, it was utilised by Jane Harrison in the early twentieth century. It was in fact developed over a century before the feminist resurgence, in the work of the Swiss sociologist J.J. Bachofen. For Bachofen, Athena was the agent of the emergent patriarchy, whose actions inaugurated the 'age of Apollo', the new stage in religion which replaced the veneration of female powers with the rule of the Olympian gods. Among the evidence adduced by Bachofen is Aeschylus' *Oresteia* where Athena's ruling in favour of Orestes, the matricide and protégé of Apollo, recalled the 'great turning-point of existence' (Bachofen 1967: 100) between matriarchy and patriarchy. In the play, Orestes avoids punishment for killing his mother, Klytaimnestra, because as Athena states, his act was in revenge for Klytaimnestra's own, more serious, murder of his father, Agamemnon. In making a judgement in favour of Orestes, Athena makes her often-quoted statement in favour of 'the male', part of which opened Chapter 1 of the present book and which I shall now quote in more detail:

> My duty is here to provide the final judgement and I shall cast my lot for Orestes. Nobody is the mother that gave birth to me, and I approve of the male in every respect, with all my heart, with the exception of undergoing marriage, and I am exceedingly of the father. Therefore I cannot award better honour to the death of the woman who killed her husband, the guardian of the house.
>
> (Aeschylus, *Eumenides* 734–9)

Athena's intervention had, on Bachofen's reading, the effect of 'usher[ing] in the victory of the higher paternity and of the heavenly light', a new stage in human progress, termed by him the 'age of Apollo' (110), after the god who defended Orestes. Athena becomes at once the agent whose actions bring about the end of matriarchy and the figure whose blend of gendered characteristics symbolises the transition to patriarchy.

'SNAKE' AND 'SHIELD GODDESS'

When Sir Arthur Evans excavated the prehellenic ('Minoan') civilisation of Bronze Age Krete in the early twentieth century, he uncovered a preponderance of female figures. The discoveries were interpreted as evidence that the Minoans were a goddess-worshipping, matrilineal people. With these discoveries, the matriarchy theory seemed to have been confirmed. One of the images unearthed was the so-called 'snake goddess', a female figure holding a serpent in either hand. Although only a small number of images of this figure were discovered, the snake goddess was hailed as a major deity of the Minoans, a goddess who combined a concern for human and animal fertility with a protective role as the guardian of the palace. These developments are of interest for the study of Athena because the snake goddess has come to be seen as a precursor of the goddess. Her various serpentine connections have been interpreted as survivals of Athena's chthonian origins, pointing to an earlier stage in religion, one that was dominated by the veneration of nature. This was, it is held, a time when a pre-patriarchal ancestress of Athena was the major deity of the religious system of the Minoan world.

The archaeological evidence also seemed to confirm that Athena's warrior traits were later acquisitions, given to the goddess in the aftermath of the patriarchal takeover. The Minoan civilisation was supplanted by that of the invading Mycenaeans in around 1450 BC. The Mycenaeans brought with them warrior deities including the so-called 'shield goddess', a helmeted female whose body was in the form of a figure-of-eight shield. To M.P. Nilsson, among the most influential of twentieth-century historians of religion, Athena was the amalgam of this deity and the Minoan snake goddess. This, for him, as for many subsequent scholars, provided a solution to the paradox of Athena, explaining the 'curious circumstance' whereby 'the Greek divinity of war is a goddess' (Nilsson 1925: 28).

The continued appeal of this historical understanding of Athena's nature may be demonstrated by Ann Baring and Jules Cashford's study of the figure of the goddess (1991). 'Looking through the Classical myth of the daughter who sprang fully armed from the head of her father, Zeus', they write, 'we can see the direct descendant of the Minoan snake goddess of over 1,000 years earlier.' Like Harrison and Millett, they regard Athena's duality as the product of a patriarchal refashioning of her nature and myth, in their words a 'deliberate revisioning of an older inheritance' which leaves 'no trace . . . of the goddess'. 'Through the image of Athena', they conclude, 'the matriarchal character of the Minoan goddess is brought into relation with the patriarchal ideals of Aryan and Dorian Greece' (Baring and Cashford 1991: 334, 337, 338).

Is it not difficult to see why these developments have had such an impact on the interpretation of Athena. Every image of her might be seen to lend itself to interpretation along the Minoan/Mycenaean or matriarchal/patriarchal lines, with her warrior aspects stemming from her Mycenaean heritage and her connections with animals and birds seemingly betraying her earlier incarnations. Scholarship on Athena has been infused with an understanding of her as the product of a primordial amalgamation of two originally separate and widely different beings. Such notions were applied to Athenian religion by C.J. Herington, for example, whose study of local manifestations of the goddess (1955) interpreted her as an amalgam of an earth goddess (Polias) and the warrior virgin (Parthenos).

CRITICISING THE MATRIARCHY MYTH

Appealing though it is, however, the matriarchy theory's potential for understanding Athena's distinctive appearance and character has been subjected to cogent criticism. The image of the warrior goddess has been traced to Minoan Krete with the identification of Minoan components in the image of the shield goddess (Rehak 1984). More broadly, the central tenet of the theory of a primordial matriarchy has come in for a sustained attack, with doubts being expressed as to whether the prevalence of feminine imagery presumes female dominance. We need only look at historical societies to realise that images of powerful females hardly provide evidence for matriarchy, the proliferation of female imagery from fifth-century Athens being a case in point. Women were notoriously marginalised in that society, but females are prominent in its art and literature, including the transgressive Amazons and Klytaimnestra and above all Athena. We might also adduce the adoration of the Virgin in Roman Catholic countries as further evidence that venerating female figures need not denote matriarchy.

With this in mind, let us return to the *Oresteia* and to Bachofen's historicist interpretation of the role of Athena. The quest for a historical kernel behind particular myths fuelled nineteenth-century interpretation of mythology but it has long since been regarded as outmoded (Hall 1996). As an interpretative model, it has been replaced by a focus upon a myth's various contexts, whether social, political or gendered. Rather than evidence for a primeval struggle between adherents of the Goddess on the one hand and god-venerating males on the other, Athena's characterisation in the *Eumenides* can be read as evidence for prevailing attitudes in fifth-century Athens towards the goddess and gender-relations. Viewed from this perspective, the representation of her can be seen to be expressing the distinctive brand of masculine femininity exhibited by the goddess, the kind that supports patriarchy in contrast to another masculine female of the *Oresteia*, Klytaimnestra. Klytaimnestra functions as a sort of mortal equivalent of Athena. Identified in the *Agamemnon* as androboulos or 'manly-minded' (11), she exhibits a quality deemed dangerous in women: intelligence. The difference is that Klytaimnestra uses her intelligence to plot against others whereas Athena's skills are used on behalf of patriarchy and institutional justice. The *Eumenides* sees her set up a lawcourt to try Orestes, the Areopagos. In the play, she also provides a model for the execution of justice by presiding over its first case.

Athena, as presented in myth, is a somewhat odd figure, with a complexly gendered persona. At the same time, she emerges as the supporter of things that are conducive to the smooth running of society. As we continue to examine myths of Athena in this book, our focus will be on their implications for understanding how she was perceived by those who possessed and transmitted the stories. In short, Athena, in myth, is 'good to think with' rather than evidence for some hypothesised prehistorical past.

WARRIOR GODDESSES OF THE ANCIENT WORLD: ANCESTRESSES OF ATHENA?

A further problem inherent in the matriarchy theory is its assumption that the possession of both warrior and feminine traits by a single goddess is something odd. To many of us, Nilsson's assessment of the feminine gender of the Greeks' war deity as something 'curious' may seem a logical one, even if we take issue with his historical solution to the question. However, even a cursory glance at the goddesses of the ancient world shows that Athena was far from unique. Among her significantly older warrior counterparts are Neith of the Egyptian city of Sais, the Semitic deities Astarte and Anat and Inanna, the love/warrior goddess of the Mesopotamian world. This section will consider the potential of looking at Athena in the light of other ancient warrior goddesses as a more feasible route to understanding her nature and functions.

From what is known about the interaction of ancient peoples and their gods, it seems reasonable to assert that, far from being the creation *ex nihilo* of the Greeks, aspects of Athena owe something at least to the goddesses of the Near East with whom she shared some of her traits. As we saw in the previous chapter, Athena's emergence from the head of Zeus may have its origins in the Mesopotamian myth of Inanna's return from the netherworld. Of all the possible ancestresses, it is Neith that has generated the most publicity, revived by Martin Bernal's investigation in the Afroasiatic origins of Greek culture.

Like Athena, Neith was a city goddess, a warrior and a patron of weaving. For Bernal Athena is, effectively, Neith in a new home. As proof, he has offered a derivation of Athena's name from 'House of Neith' (Ht Nt), the sacred name of the city of Sais, Neith's cult centre. Like other etymologies that he presents in his work, however, this one has come in for criticism from specialists in etymology, notably J. Jasanoff and A. Nussbaum (1996), who point to its reliance upon superficial likeness rather than conforming to any established sound Greek laws. Bernal's theory, it emerges from Jasanoff and Nussbaum, takes us no closer to solving the riddle of her name. It may as well be derived, they argue, from the Anatolian city Adana or the Carthaginian goddess Tanit or even, applying Bernal's own methodology, a feminised version of Satan.

A recent attempt at seeking Athena's early development is Annette Teffeteller's (2001) proposed connection between Athena and a Hittite warrior goddess, a deity known as the Sungoddess of Arinna after her major cult centre. The Sungoddess' appearances in the Annals of the Hittite kings dating from the seventeenth century BC show her to be a deity who shares certain of the traits of the much younger Athena, notably a connection with rulers and their people. The first of the kings, Hattusili I (*c.* 1650–20), for example, is described as 'beloved' of her, while Mursili II (*c.* 1322–1295) celebrated her assistance on campaigns that enabled the people to 'rage against the surrounding lands like a lion'. Teffeteller even moots the possibility that Athena's name may be derived from the sun goddess in that Arinna as a place-name might have been borrowed by Greek speakers in Anatolia who will have heard it as Atana, the form in which Athena's name seems to appear in the Linear B tablets from Krete in the middle of the second millennium (Chapter 6).

Teffeteller's account of Athena's origins has implications for determining the role of borrowings from Anatolia upon the forma-tion of Greek religion. As I should like to consider, however, even if Athena has her origins in an earlier goddess, she will have evolved beyond her origins to suit the developing needs of the Greeks. The introduction of a deity into the pantheon of a new people would not have involved the passive acceptance of that deity but would have led to the deity being adapted to suit the new circumstances. As we saw in the case of Athena's birth (Chapter 1), Mesopotamian, and possibly Hittite, motifs are apparent, but rather than being adopted wholesale, they have been adapted in their new context to depict a distinctively Greek goddess, the head-born daughter of Zeus who resolves the succession problem and upholds her father's rule. The Greeks developed in a distinctive manner among the peoples of the Near East. It seems not unreasonable to assert that their gods would have developed in ways that suited the needs of the worshipping group.

Athena's attributes and functions may well be borrowings from the Hittites or other earlier peoples, but she would have meant something substantially different to the Greeks than, say, the sun goddess of Arinna did to the Hittites or Inanna did to the Mesopotamians. The eighth century BC, when Greece emerged out of the Dark Ages with an alphabet, a religion and a literature, saw the development of the polis, unique as a system of political and social organisation in the ancient world. Of all the Greek deities, Athena is especially connected with this institution. The poliad deity *par excellence*, her principal place of worship was the akropolis from where she functioned as the armed protectress of the city. In this role, which we will investigate in some depth in our chapters on Athenian religion and on Athena cults in the wider Greek world, there may be echoes of the earlier protectress of the Hittite kings, but if so, she will have been transformed in the process as befitted the peculiar local circumstances of the Greek world. Athena has elements in common with other goddesses, but if we attempt to seek a perfect fit, we are asking the wrong questions.

OVERVIEW

The desire to identify Athena's origins continues to excite interest, but there has been no wholly satisfactory solution. The 'conventional view' about the Greek gods expressed in Hurwit's comment quoted at the head of this chapter holds true for Athena, the problem being that the identity of this 'somewhere else' remains largely obscure. The theory that her origins can be traced to a hypothetical matriarchal prehistory looks outmoded from a scholarly perspective, as does the notion that she was an amalgam of a peaceful prehellenic deity and the war goddess of the invading Greeks. Athena shares characteristics of numerous older warrior goddesses, including the Hittite Sungoddess, but there is insufficient evidence to enable any conclusive conclusions.

In the next chapter we will consider how, if the quest for Athena's origins leaves us largely frustrated, we are to make sense of the goddess and her multifaceted nature.

3

FROM ORIGINS TO FUNCTIONS: ATHENA IN THE PANTHEON

What pleases her are wars and the things done by Ares, battles and fighting, as well as the preparation of splendid pieces of craftsmanship. She was the first to teach mortal craftsmen to make war-chariots and other chariots wrought in bronze and it is she who teaches soft-skinned young women inside the house the skill of making splendid pieces of craftsmanship, putting it firmly into the minds of each.

(*Homeric Hymn to Aphrodite* 10–16)

INTRODUCTION: CONFRONTING THE PANTHEON

The major Greek gods have such distinctive characteristics and functions that it is tempting to study each of them in isolation – to produce a detailed study of, say, Zeus in his various incarnations and guises, or Apollo, Aphrodite or Athena, who is particularly appealing in this regard due to her distinctive appearance, the various festivals connected with her and her numerous epithets, modes of operation and attributes. Scholarship of recent decades, however, has stressed the dangers associated with such an approach, because it risks overlooking the importance of one of the principal features of ancient Greek religion: the pantheon. This chapter will be concerned with the question of how we should steer a path between, on the one hand, Athena's distinctive character and functions and on the other, her status as one divinity among many in the polytheistic religion of the Greeks.

THE 'NEW WAY': THE FUNCTIONALIST PARADIGM

A significant concern in the nineteenth and early to mid-twentieth centuries was to produce studies of the major gods that traced the salient characteristics of each: their epithets for example, the sanctuaries at which they were worshipped and their festivals. The most distinguished example of this, L.R. Farnell's five-volume *Cults of the Greek States* (1896–1909), presents a detailed account of the major deities, cataloguing their cult, cult-monuments and ideal types. It remains a valuable reference work, especially in Athena's case, for its geographical register of her cults (Farnell 1896: 419–23), but now looks out of date, because it is of limited value for providing a sense of how the gods were thought to interact with one another. It presents, effectively, a 'Zeus religion', an 'Athena religion', an 'Apollo religion' etc. (cf. Burkert 1985: 216) rather than an account of how the Greeks experienced their gods as beings within a polytheistic system, each with particular roles and characteristics, but none operating in isolation.

The study of the Greek gods has been transformed through the work of a group of francophone scholars, often identified as the 'Paris School', who have sought to understand deities via their place in the pantheon. As set out in the work of one of the most influential, Jean-Pierre Vernant:

> We must analyse the structure of the pantheon and show how the various powers are grouped, associated together and opposed to and distinguished from each other. Only in this way can the pertinent features of each god or each group of gods emerge.
>
> (1979: 99).

This approach, influenced by the structuralist methodology developed by the French anthropologist Claude Lévi-Strauss is highly appealing as a means of interpreting Athena. It frees us from the need to study her in terms of her prehistorical formation, and enables us to look, instead, at the particular contexts in which she was thought to manifest herself. In works by Vernant, Marcel

Detienne and others, a series of oppositions have been established with a series of other gods, where she consistently brings to bear skill, technical aptitude, and, above all, metis. These qualities have been seen to underlie her interventions in myth and cult, and are regarded as pivotal to an interpretation of her areas of competence. The influence of the functionalist paradigm is exemplified in Walter Burkert's summary of Athena's functions:

> Poseidon violently sires the horse, Athena bridles it and builds the chariot; Hermes may multiply the flocks, Athena teaches the use of wool. Even in war, Athena is no exponent of derring-do – this is captured in the figure of Ares – but cultivates the war-dance, tactics and discipline.

> (1985: 141)

We will explore this methodology by presenting several case studies, each of which looks at her relationship with one of her fellow gods. Our starting point will be Poseidon, as it is this relationship that has generated particular interest from a structuralist perspective. Sometimes, as we shall see, the standard way of interpreting Athena through the lens of structuralism is limited as a means of shedding light upon her modes of operation. Although applicable up to a point, the metis/elemental force opposition is overly limiting in certain contexts because Athena is herself depicted as a being with powers that might be termed 'elemental'. Through restructuring the model, however, we will see that the methodology provides a useful vehicle for exploring Athena's nature and divine relationships.

ATHENA AND POSEIDON: THE HORSE AND THE SEA

It is in the case of Athena's common areas of concern with Poseidon that the structuralist opposition on the face of it works particularly effectively. In his various areas of competence, Poseidon is a volatile god, given to displays of anger and ferocity, who seems very different from the skilful and intelligent Athena. He is the earth-shaker, for example, and the bringer of floods, whose ability to cause destruction may be exemplified by his response to the Athenians' rejection of him in favour of Athena, when in his anger he floods the Attic plain (see Chapter 5).

The contrast between the two deities is discernible in one of their shared areas of activity, horsemanship. As Poseidon Hippios and Athena Hippia they are each deities 'of the horse', but Athena has been identified as a power of metis in contrast to the elemental power that her fellow god brings to bear. Poseidon is the horse god *par excellence*, who fathered the first ever creature by ejaculating on a rock, while among his other offspring were the fabulous horses Pegasos (one of his children with Medusa) and Areion, whom he fathered on Demeter Erinys ('Fury'), when he raped her in the guise of a stallion. Athena's interventions, in contrast, involve skill and technology. As set out in the *Homeric Hymn to Aphrodite* quoted at the head of this chapter, she was 'the first to teach mortal craftsmen to make war-chariots and other chariots wrought in bronze'. She also enabled Bellerophon to tame Pegasos, Poseidon's son, by presenting him with the bit (Pindar, *Olympian* 13.75–8). The structuralist opposition between the two gods provides a means of understanding the different abilities that each possesses. Poseidon is the horse's creator, while Athena tames it and makes it useful to mankind. When she herself plays a part in the creation of a horse, indeed, it is not a living creature but the Trojan Horse, the ultimate instance of artifice, technology and trickery (see further Chapter 4).

When we turn to the sea, however, the structuralist opposition works less well as a means of contrasting Poseidon as an elemental force with Athena as a power of civilisation and metis. Poseidon was the major sea god of the Greeks. Athena, too, was venerated as a maritime power, worshipped as Promachorma ('guardian of the anchorage') for example, on a promontory called Bouporthmos ('ox crossing') in the Argolid and as Koryphasia on the Koryphasion promontory near Pylos. Her best-known maritime cult, meanwhile, at Cape Sounion on the southern tip of Attica, was situated on a low hill below the sanctuary of Poseidon Soter ('safety').

The metis/elemental force opposition applies in relation to the sea, but only to a point. Of vital importance to a seafaring people like the Greeks, the sea was regarded as violent, dangerous and 'desolate' (*atrugetos*). These qualities were reflected in the nature of the god who was assigned the sea as his domain at the time when the world was being divided up between him and Zeus, who acquired the sky, and Hades, who became lord of the underworld. Like his brothers, he was at once the power who controlled his designated domain and intimately associated with that domain. When he rode across it in the *Iliad*, 'it parted before him, rejoicing' (13.29), but when he was angry, the sea was destructive and potentially deadly, as Odysseus discovered after he incurred the god's wrath in *Odyssey* for blinding another of his sons, the cyclops Polyphemos. When Athena intervenes in connection with the sea, in contrast, it is often to promote skilled activities including shipbuilding, navigation and helmsmanship. She built the first ever ship, variously identified as that of Jason or of Danaos (Apollodoros 2.1.4), and was responsible for the ship that brought Helen to Troy (Homer, *Iliad* 5.59). In the most famous epic voyage, Jason and the Argonauts' journey to Colchis to capture the Golden Fleece, she selected the trees for the Argo, chose the pilot and supervised the shipbuilding (Apollonius Rhodius, *Argonautica* 1.18–19; 109ff.). She intervened during the voyage too, nowhere more strikingly than during the clashing rocks incident, when she helped the ship through at just the right moment (2.598ff.). She also assisted Odysseus' son Telemachos on his quest for news of his father (Homer, *Odyssey* 1.113ff) by advising him on the sort of ship to equip, guiding him during his journey and generating a favourable wind to Pylos.

Athena is represented as capable of operating in a manner that differs from her fellow sea god, intervening to help skilled practitioners and seafarers to create a path through Poseidon's domain. Yet to characterise her solely as a goddess of metis would be to oversimplify her role as a maritime power. She is herself able to control conditions at sea and capable of generating storms no less powerful and destructive than any of Poseidon's. When she sprang from Zeus's head, 'the sea moved and frothed with dark waves, while foam suddenly burst forth' (*Homeric Hymn* 28.11–13). Likewise, in her fury at the Greeks' sacrilege during the sack of Troy, she produced the storm that devastated the returning fleet (Chapter 4).

With Athena capable of operating in a way that affects conditions at sea, the standard structuralist opposition between Athena (metis) and Poseidon (elemental force) emerges as overly limited as a means of accounting for Athena's distinctive mode of activity. But far from making us desirous of writing off structuralist methodology, our survey has demonstrated its potential to elucidate Athena's particular traits. Comparing the two deities in their maritime guises uncovers an intriguing contrast between them. Poseidon's operations are guided by his role as an elemental force. Athena, in contrast brings to bear a duality between the 'civiliser' of the sea who promotes skilled activities and the power able to create violent storms.

The value of the structuralist methodology is that it confirms what we have already identified as a distinctive quality of Athena, namely that there is a particular duality about her. On the one hand, she is a civiliser, who brings orders and who resolves various situations. But she is also capable of generating disorder and chaos. We will now test the implications of the approach further though an investigation of another of Athena's divine relationships, that with Hephaistos.

ATHENA AND HEPHAISTOS: SKILLED CRAFT

The god of fire, blacksmiths and artisans, Hephaistos was so closely linked with fire that his very name could denote the element. This is similar in part to how Poseidon is intimately linked with the sea, except that Hephaistos is a god endowed with metis, in his case a cunning that elevated him beyond a solely elemental power. He is fire, but he is also a craftsman able to exploit and tame fire. As klutometis ('renowned for cunning'), he was responsible for works of exceptional skill including the shield of Achilleus, certain golden-wheeled tripods that were capable of moving by themselves and automata fashioned from gold to assist him in his forge. It was thanks to Hephaistos that the birth of Athena was able to take place, when he freed her from the body of Zeus with his 'child-delivering axe' (Kallimachos fragment 37). He also created a throne for his mother Hera that was gleaming and enticing, but from which she could not escape until he released her from the invisible constraints that were imprisoning her. This takes us to another dimension of his cunning. He was an outsider among the gods – the lame god, detested by his mother as soon as he was born (Chapter 1) – but he was able to use his skills to extract revenge. This ability is seen most notably when he takes revenge on Aphrodite by trapping her with her lover Ares in a net so fine that it was invisible (Homer, *Odyssey* 8.266ff.). So effective is his trickery and artifice that it could trap even the goddess of the wiles of love.

Athena, too, was able to fashion intricate objects, in her case as a woolworker. One of her epithets was Ergane ('worker') and she is sometimes depicted holding woolworking implements. According to one ancient description of the palladion, for example, 'in the right hand it held a spear lifted up, while in the other, a distaff and spindle' (Apollodoros 3.12.3). In her contest with the mortal weaver Arachne, she produced a tapestry with 'subtle delicate tints that change insensibly from shade to shade' (Ovid, *Metamorphoses* 6.63–4, tr. Melville). In the *Iliad*, she is clothed in the dress that she herself wove (5.734–5) and in one version of the creation of the aegis, the flayed skin of the giant Pallas provides the raw material for her techne (Apollodoros 1.6.2). As well as weaving her own clothes, she was the patron of mortal woolworkers, whether women who performed the task as domestic labour, such as the 'soft-skinned young women' of the *Homeric Hymn to Aphrodite* quoted at the head of this chapter – who carried out their skill inside their houses – or those who did it as their trade. Several of the epigrams in the *Palatine Anthology* concern professional spinsters who dedicate their tools to Athena as their patron. In 6.288, for example, four sisters dedicate their implements to her as a proportion of their profit, and to pray for enhanced prosperity, while in 6.289, three sisters dedicate their implements on the occasion of their retirement.

Athena is associated with other skilled activities too. As well as helping to create the Trojan Horse, she fashioned the palladion in the likeness of a childhood friend called Pallas (Apollodoros 3.12.3). She was the patron of potters and shared Hephaistos' function as deity of metalwork, the difference being that she did not herself work with metal. When she required weapons, she turned to

Hephaistos, just as all the gods did. This differentiation provides a way of understanding the differing status of Athena and Hephaistos among the gods. As we have seen, Hephaistos was the divine servant, a figure of fun, whose status was peripheral in contrast to that of Athena, the goddess who was, in the words of Hera, 'distinguished among all the blessed gods' (*Homeric Hymn to Pythian Apollo* 315), a contrast that reflects the status of metalworkers in Greek society as essential to society, but marginalised and even feared. Athena had the technical ability to teach skills and promote male craft, but she did not, herself, work with these materials.

The main differences we have identified so far, then, are that while both deities are gods of craft, the works of Hephaistos are fashioned in the noise of the furnace while Athena does not get her hands dirty, as it were. Her particular skill, woolworking, was, in contrast, the consummate female activity for a society where the proper role for women was working at the loom. This division of labour is reflected in their respective roles in the creation of Pandora, where Hephaistos used base material (clay) and Athena taught her woolworking:

> He [Zeus] urged renowned Hephaistos to make haste and mix earth with water and to put in it the voice and strength of humankind, and fashion a sweet, lovely maiden-shape, like to the immortal goddesses in face; and Athena to teach her needlework and the weaving of the varied web.
>
> (Hesiod, *Works and Days* 60–64, Loeb translation, slightly adapted)

So far we have been highlighting the distinctive manner of operation of the two deities. As the male and female deities of craft, however, they are frequently paired and accorded similar manners of operating. In a simile in *Odyssey* 6, they are each envisaged as teaching 'all kinds of skill' to 'some skilful man', enabling him to produce 'graceful' (*charieis*) work (6.232–4). Their close associations in Athens reflect the importance of craft in the city, particularly their connection at the Hephaisteion above the Agora, where Athena was even known as Hephaisteia ('of Hephaistos'). The Chalkeia, in honour of both gods, was the festival of smiths. It was also the occasion when the loom was set up for the Panathenaic peplos. In other words, male craft and women's work were jointly honoured in the cult of Athena and Hephaistos.

As deities of craft, Athena and Hephaistos had in common a concern with the promotion of civilisation. One of the Orphic hymns, for example, envisages 'Athena presiding over various arts, in particular that of weaving, and Hephaistos especially to watch over other skills' (Kern, *Orphica Fragmenta* 178). This joint benefaction is taken a stage further in the *Homeric Hymn to Hephaistos* where they are envisaged as enabling mankind to become civilised because they 'taught men glorious crafts throughout the world: men who previously dwelt in caves in the mountains like wild beasts' (20). Such notions may lie behind the Athenian foundation myth concerning the birth of one of the early kings, Erichthonios:

> Athena came to Hephaistos wanting him to fashion arms. But he, having been rejected by Aphrodite, began to desire Athena and started to pursue her, but she fled. When he came near her with a great deal of distress – for he was lame – he attempted to have sex with her; but she, being chaste and a parthenos would not suffer him to act thus, and he ejaculated onto the leg of the goddess. In disgust, she wiped off the semen with wool, and threw it on the ground; and as she fled and the semen fell on the ground, Erichthonios was born.
>
> (Apollodoros 3.14.6)

One aspect of this multifaceted story (to be explored further in Chapter 5) concerns the ability of Hephaistos and Athena to produce a child in circumstances that should have precluded it. Hephaistos' near-magical ability to create extraordinary things is evident in his mixing of semen and earth to produce Erichthonios. What distinguishes Erichthonios' origins, however, is the mediation of Athena. Elsewhere Hephaistos' creative partner, here she becomes in a sense his sexual partner too when she wipes the semen off her leg and casts it on the ground. Erichthonios was even, in one ancient derivation of his name, 'Woolly-Earthy' (*erion-chthonios*: Etymologicum Magnum sv. *Erechtheus*; Scholia on Homer, *Iliad* 4.8). He is, here, the product of the earth that Hephaistos is capable of utilising to fashion living beings and also the wool used by Athena in her own skilled work.

Applying structuralist methodology to investigate the relationship between Athena and Hephaistos in their shared field of operation provides a way of understanding Athena's mode of operation as a deity of skilled craft. She is the cult partner – and even in a sense the sexual partner – of Hephaistos, sharing his role as a patron of techne and being, like him, imbued with metis in a practical sense. Through her patronage of skilled craft, Athena emerges once again as a benefactor of civilisation, possessed of technical skill and passing this ability to mankind. This demonstrates further that the structuralist methodology does not have to rely solely upon opposition, but can also shed light on the modes of operations of pairs of deities with comparable areas of expertise.

ATHENA AND ARES: WAR

It has become a near-cliché to differentiate between Ares as the embodiment of war's violent and chaotic aspects, and Athena as the goddess who orders and systemises it through inventions like the chariot and the armed dance. In the nineteenth century, John Ruskin stated that Ares is 'brutal muscular strength' while Athena represents 'the strength of young lives passed in pure air and swift exercise' (1890: 49). The contrast has resurfaced in structuralist-influenced research with the differences between taken to reflect the ideals of Greek warfare (e.g. Daraki 1980). Ares has been said to stand for the kind of violent behaviour that warriors ought to avoid, while Athena represents war as warriors are supposed to fight it. Ares signals the hubris of the warrior who attempts to pit himself against the gods; Athena is the one who inspires *menos* ('strength', 'courage' or 'prowess').

It is possible to identify similarities between the two deities, however, that undermine these rather neat patterns, for in order to inspire *menos*, Athena operates in ways that are resonant of Ares. She is a warmonger from the moment she is born shaking her armour and making her war cry (Chapter 1). She displays ferocity in the battle between the gods and giants, even flaying Pallas, and as we have seen, fashioning the aegis from his skin. This section will

explore some of her warlike traits and interventions in order to
determine how far the structualist view of Athena as the power of
civilisation and metis applies in this instance.

In the *Iliad*, Athena gets into the thick of battle to assist her
favourites. The extraordinary *menos* of Diomedes that dominates
Book 5 is inspired by the goddess (e.g. 5.1–8). At one point he displays such unbridled rage under Athena's influence that no one,
neither Greek nor Trojan, is able to discern who he is or even
which side he is on as he 'storm[s] up the plain like a winter torrent'
(87–8). This could not be more different from the usual pattern
of battle in the epic, where warriors are aware of the identity and
pedigree of their opponents. Indeed, Diomedes himself otherwise exhibits such self-control that he refrains from combat with
the Trojan Glaukos because their ancestors were guest-friends
(6.212–31).

With Athena's help, another of her favourites, Achilleus, also
takes on an appearance that differs from the usual pattern of heroic
conduct when she clothes him in the aegis, places a golden cloud
around his head and makes fire blaze from him (18.203–18). He then
utters a war cry and she adds her own to it and the results are
extraordinary: 'unutterable confusion' ensues (218) and the panic
produces deaths through 'friendly fire': the only instance of this in
the *Iliad*. With Athena's ability to inspire such extreme warrior
behaviour, it is her similarities with Ares that are brought to the fore.
Indeed, the *Iliad* frequently describes the gods in comparable terms,
even though their relationship is presented as less than amiable,
witness for instance Ares' complaint to Zeus about the favouritism
shown to Athena (chapter 1). The shield of Achilles, for example,
includes a representation of defenders of a town under siege sallying
out led by Athena and Ares: 'each golden, dressed in golden garments, beautiful and great in their armour' (18.516–17). The shorter
of the two *Homeric Hymns to Athena* (11.2–3) sums up the relationship. Athena is 'terrible' it says, 'and with Ares she makes her
business the works of war, the sack of cities and the shouting and
the battle'.

But there is always a degree of difference. Homeric heroes
become the 'equal of Ares' in the thick of battle. When Athena

intervenes it is intimacy rather than identification that is produced. She is the deity who leads the warrior by the hand (4.541–2) in a way that one could not imagine Ares doing. Moreover, unlike Ares, Athena is able to distance herself from war and violence. In the *Iliad* (5.733ff.), she arms herself for battle by removing the self-made dress that she had been wearing, and replacing it with weapons, most strikingly, the 'terrible tasselled aegis' which contains the personified abstractions Phobos (Fear), Eris (Strife), Alke (Strength), blood-chilling Ioke (Pursuit), and then, most of all 'the head of the terrible monster the Gorgon, both fearful and awful to look on'. These abstractions become part of the spectacle she produces; but they are also detachable.

Ares, meanwhile, has a more permanent kind of attachment with some of these figures: Phobos and Eris are even his relatives, since he is identified as the father of the former (e.g. *Iliad* 13.299), and the brother of the latter (*Iliad* 4.441). Perhaps what we have here is a contrast between armour and natural forces. The opposition between the deities is not so much between war as a cosmic, destructive force and 'civilised warfare' as between natural power and weaponry. It is Athena's weapons coupled with her frenzied cry and blazing eyes that make her a deity of war and she possesses power that she could either use or turn off. Ares, meanwhile, is more closely identified with his warlike power, as may be exemplified by the description of the two gods in the Hesiodic *Shield of Herakles* (191–200). 'There', the poem recounts, 'was baneful Ares the spoil-wearer himself. In his hands he held a spear and he was urging on his foot-soldier, and he was red with blood'. 'There, too', the poem continues, 'was the daughter of Zeus, bringer of spoil [*ageleiē*], Tritogeneia. She seemed as though she intended to arm herself for battle, since she held a spear in her hand, and a golden helmet, and the aegis about her shoulders.' In certain respects, they are described in comparable terms. Ares is the 'spoil-wearer' and Athena the 'bringer of spoil', but while Ares is covered in blood, Athena is clothed in armour.

Ares is little more than the god of war. Athena is warlike when she needs to be, but she is much more besides. This may be exemplified by figure 4, the other side of figure 2, the image we discussed in

Figure 4 Herakles and the Nemean Lion, Attic black-figure amphora, Virginia Museum of Fine Arts, Richmond 60.23. The Arthur and Margaret Glasgow Fund. Photo: Katherine Wetzel. © Virginia Museum of Fine Arts.

Chapter 1, where we see a very different-looking Athena from the resplendent goddess emerging in her warrior panoply out of the head of Zeus. Armed only with her spear, she makes an intriguing contrast to Herakles' mortal helper Iolaos who is kitted out in full panoply.

The standard way of evaluating Athena's interventions in war is too limiting. However, this far from invalidates the structuralist methodology of comparing and contrasting pairs of deities. The comparison brings out Athena's particular manner of operation as a warrior, intervening to assist her favourites and able to inspire their displays of warrior power, while deriving her power from her weapons rather than some natural affinity with war of the kind exemplified by Ares.

OVERVIEW: A KEY TO ATHENA?

The result of this survey is a picture of Athena as a multifaceted goddess with numerous functions including seamanship, horse-manship, craft and war. Our discussion has shed further light too on the nature of Athena's metis, which is capable of transforming things that are raw, dangerous and elemental into useful objects, including such unlikely raw materials as the dead body of Pallas and the wool she was carrying when Hephaistos attempted to have sex with her. Through our investigation of her role within the pantheon, she has emerged as a power of technology and creativity who pro-motes creativity and order, but with another side to her power, that of the storm bringer and warmonger.

Exploring the structuralist approach in relation to Athena has furthered our understanding of some of her distinctive traits. It has also shown how she functioned within the amalgamation of gods that was the pantheon. There was no separate 'Athena religion'. She functioned as part of a network of beings so that in various fields of competence, she was variously compared and contrasted to her fellow divine beings.

4

HEROES, HEROINES AND THE TROJAN WAR

The gods we have as allies are not worse than those of the Argives, my lord. For Hera is their champion, Zeus's wife, but Athena is ours. This too is a source of good fortune for us, that we have better gods. For Pallas Athena will not put up with defeat.

(Sophocles, *Children of Herakles* 347–52, tr. Kovacs)

INTRODUCTION: HELPING FRIENDS, HARMING ENEMIES

Athena appears in an extraordinary range of myths, due in part to her role as the patron of heroes. She participates in stories associated with numerous heroes, from the Greek warriors at Troy to the great adventurers including Jason, Perseus and above all Herakles. So pervasive is her role that it might even be said that one of the 'qualifications' for heroism in Greek myth was to have Athena on one's side. W. F. Otto memorably identified Athena as the 'goddess of nearness' (1954). It is in her interventions in the lives of heroes that this characterisation has particular resonance.

There was a flip side to this protection and assistance, however. As well as the greatest friend that a hero might acquire, she was, as we shall see, a fierce and persistent victimiser of any mortal she regarded as her enemy. This is something easy to overlook. It is the kind of role we tend to associate with certain of her fellow deities: Hera, for example, or Poseidon, whose victimisation of Odysseus is one of the driving forces of the hero's myth. But, in fact, those who incurred Athena's displeasure suffered devastating consequences. Ajax, for example, had been one of her favourites until, one time when she appeared before him on the battlefield at Troy, he dismissed her, claiming that with his prodigious strength, he did not require her assistance (Sophocles, *Ajax* 770–6).

Her victimisation of Ajax is unrelenting and even shocking. After driving him mad in the aftermath of the contest for the arms of Achilles, she sends him into the Greek camp thinking that he is killing Odysseus and the other Greeks while all the time he is slaughtering their cattle. He becomes, through Athena's intervention, a pathetic, deluded figure whose shame leads ultimately to his suicide. Odysseus is capable of pity at the spectacle of the deluded hero:

> I pity his wretchedness, though he is my enemy, for the terrible yoke of blindness that is on him.
>
> (Sophocles, *Ajax* 121–3, tr. Moore)

Athena in contrast is merciless:

> To laugh at your enemies – what sweeter laughter can there be than that?
>
> (78–9, tr. Moore)

As well as looking at Athena as the helper of heroes who uses her powers on behalf of her favourites, we will be tracing her role as a victimiser, not only of individuals, but also of whole groups. The Trojans, as we will see, incur her displeasure to such a degree that she brings about the city's fall. So, in turn, do the Greeks, when in the aftermath of the Trojan War, she turns against them *en masse*. Finally, we will examine Athena's relationship with heroines of myth. While capable of closeness, even tenderness, with heroes, she falls out with or causes suffering for a range of females. A brief examination of her associations with young mythic women will enable us to discern further how the Greeks understood her as a female deity.

HEROES ON QUESTS

Far from home in strange and often unfriendly lands, various heroes on quests were able, with Athena's help, to overcome various difficulties in their paths. We saw in the previous chapter how she helped Bellerophon to tame Pegasos by providing him with the bit and how, under her tutelage, Jason was prepared for his journey to Colchis to get the golden fleece. Most of the sources provide Jason with a mortal helper once he has reached Colchis, the local princess Medea whose love for the visitor led her to betray her family on his behalf. Figure 5, however, from a red-figure kylix by Douris of c. 480–70 BC, depicts Athena watching over the hero as he is being disgorged by the dragon guarding the fleece.

Another hero, Perseus, would have been at a loss without Athena. Before embarking on his quest, Perseus was an impetuous young man who offered Polydektes, his mother's suitor, the head of the Gorgon as a wedding present. Once he had been dispatched to the land of the Gorgon, Athena made an appearance before him, in this instance with an accomplice, the travellers' god, Hermes. The gods provided him with winged sandals that enabled him to fly to the land inhabited by Medusa and her sisters and subsequently to flee with her severed head. He was given a scimitar to cut off the head and a bag to place it in to ensure that he would not inadvertently be petrified by her gaze. He was also permitted to borrow the cap of invisibility of Hades. Another gift of Athena was a mirror that enabled him to see the reflection of the monster without looking directly into her eyes.

In her benefactions for Perseus, Athena intervenes as a power of metis. Each object reverses his position as a lone mortal in a land inhabited by monsters, enabling him to succeed in a strange place where strength alone would have been useless. With her power to petrify, Medusa ought to have been invulnerable, but under Athena's guidance, Perseus beheads her, flees the scene invisible in his cap and returns to the civilised world wearing a further gift, the winged sandals. Athena does not make Perseus' task an easy one: instead she enables him to succeed where the odds would otherwise have been stacked against him.

Figure 5 Jason being disgorged by the dragon, observed by Athena; Attic red-figure cup from Cervetri by Douris; Rome, Vatican 16545; redrawn by S.J. Deacy.

ODYSSEUS AND HERAKLES

While Perseus' achievements would have been impossible without Athena's assistance, Odysseus and Herakles succeed in part by drawing upon their own resources. The prodigious strength of Herakles, in evidence as he carries out his numerous feats of strength and endurance, is seen from childhood when he strangles the serpents sent by Hera to kill him in his cot. His exploits make the careers of Perseus et al. seem bland in comparison, centred as these are around a single exploit. Herakles' victims include monsters that ought to have been invulnerable – the Nemean Lion with its impenetrable skin for example, and the Hydra with its re-growing heads. As the hero who 'wandered endlessly over the boundless earth and sea' (*Homeric Hymn to Herakles* 4–5), his travels exceed those of any hero, taking him even as far as underworld to capture Kerberos.

As for Odysseus, he is able to draw on the cunning that leads him to be 'forever' as the *Odyssey* describes it, 'using to every advantage the mind that was in him' (13.255, tr. Lattimore). He is responsible, for example, for the ploy that enabled Troy to be taken: 'the stratagem great Odysseus filled once with men and brought into the upper city' (8.493–5, Lattimore translation, slightly adapted). His interactions with others are characterised by caution, as Athena notes with near frustration when she appears before him in Ithaka in *Odyssey* 13. He is, as she puts it, 'full of wiles, never tiring of deceit', a man who, even back in his homeland, continues to employ the 'trickery and . . . deceitful stories', which are 'dear to you to your very essence' (291–5).

On the face of it, Odysseus and Herakles appear to be less in need of divine assistance than the likes of Perseus and Jason. The *Odyssey* even depicts Odysseus as Athena's mortal equivalent, whose use of cunning has a parallel in Athena's reputation on Olympos. Athena states:

> You are by far the best of men for counsel and for stories, and I among the gods am famed for wit and skill.

> (13.297–9)

But in fact, both heroes receive repeated help from Athena. Examining Athena's patronage of Odysseus and then Herakles will enable us to investigate what amounts almost to a paradox of hero myth: the greater the hero, the more he merits divine assistance.

Odysseus is among the heroes who benefit from Athena's help at

Troy (e.g. *Odyssey* 13.314–18). She goes to particular trouble, too, to assist him in his attempts to return to Ithaka after the Trojan War, intervening with Zeus on his behalf (e.g. *Odyssey* 1.44ff.) even though this potentially brings her into conflict with Odysseus' divine enemy, Poseidon. When, at certain points in the *Odyssey*, he thinks that he is relying wholly on his own powers, Athena is in fact in proximity, assisting him secretly. Shipwrecked on the island of the Phaiakians, for example, Odysseus uses his charm to get the local princess, Nausikaa, on his side (6.145 ff.). He subsequently wins over her people too (7.139) even though they are, by nature, wary of strangers. All the time, however, Athena has been intervening on his behalf. The encounter with Nausikaa only occurred because Athena appeared to the girl in a dream (6.13 ff.), telling her to go with her companions to the river where Odysseus was lying shipwrecked. While he was using his powers to win over Nausikaa, Athena transformed his appearance to make him more handsome and taller (6.229–35). She used her transformative power to endear him to the Phaiakians as well (8.18–23).

Athena's interventions in relation to Odysseus are at the other extreme from the notion of heroic achievement proffered by Ajax, who missed the point of Athena as a divine benefactor. Her interventions enhance the accomplishments of her favourites, elevating rather than compromising their heroism.

Herakles benefits even more than Odysseus does from Athena's assistance. 'I frequently saved him', she recalls in the *Iliad*, 'when he was worn out by his struggles under Eurystheus' (8.362). While he is dying in agony in Sophocles' *Trachiniae*, he cries to Athena in his suffering (1031). Athena's presence is a regular feature of visual depictions of his labours and other achievements. Vase paintings, including figure 4 above, frequently show her observing his actions, while the best-known representation of the twelve labours, the metopes on the temple of Zeus at Olympia (see, e.g., Carpenter 1991: fig. 173), include Athena in four of the scenes, variously observing, providing companionship and actively assisting her protégé. In the first metope, for example, she is looking on as Herakles stands victorious over the Nemean Lion. A girlish, rather passive figure, she is holding a spear but lacking any other warrior attributes, as in figure 4. In the tenth, in contrast, Athena is actively helping Herakles to hold up the sky by standing behind him, sharing the burden.

The degree of assistance provided by Athena for Herakles throughout his heroic career is extraordinary. She assists him even when he enters into conflict with the gods: with Apollo when he tries to steal the Delphic tripod, and with Ares, when, with her assistance, he kills Ares' son Kyknos, and then enters into direct conflict with the god himself. According to the Hesiodic *Shield of Herakles*, such is her support for the hero that she intervenes to save his life during this incident, when Ares throws a spear at him, and she turns aside its force (451–6).

With her support for Herakles, Athena is the complement of another goddess, Hera. The enmity of his stepmother is evident even before his birth, when she extended Alkmene's labour to ensure that his cousin, Eurystheus, would be born before him and become king of Argos instead. After his birth, she continued her victimisation by sending the serpents to kill him in his cot. But from early on in his life, Herakles is aided in his attempts to deal with the challenges thrown in his way by Hera by the interventions of Athena, whose assistance in one story (Diodorus Siculus 4.9.6–7) even involves Athena's using her cunning ability against her fellow goddess. Fearing the wrath of Hera, Alkmene abandoned the new-born Herakles. The two goddesses passed by the exposed child and Athena persuaded Hera to suckle him, providing him with the nourishment that as a virgin she was incapable of supplying.

Athena's support of Herakles during his career as a hero culminates in his apotheosis, where, with her help, he crosses the normally closed divide between humanity and divinity. In a two-staged development, he was first driven, with Athena at the reins, by chariot from earth to Olympos. Subsequently, he was introduced by Athena to Zeus, his father and about-to-be fellow divinity (figure 6). This transition was one that few heroes made. Even others of Athena's favourites, set aside by her for immortalisation, failed at the final hurdle. Tydeus, one of the 'seven against Thebes' and father of Diomedes, was if anything more beloved of Athena even than his son (Chapter 3). When he was lying fatally wounded on the

Figure 6 Athena introduces Herakles to Zeus, Attic black-figure cup, London, British Museum B 424.

battlefield, Athena decided to make him immortal. The gift was withdrawn at the last moment when, in a final act of revenge against his dead rival, Melanippos, Tydeus began to eat his brains (Apollodoros 3.6.8). This act so offended Athena that she withdrew her gift. In the case of Athena's 'child' Erichthonios (see further, Chapter 5), meanwhile, the immortalisation process was already under way when two of the daughters of Kekrops peered inside the chest containing him. Once interrupted, Erichthonios remained mortal and Athena was left, instead, with a human infant to raise.

Herakles, however, makes a successful transition. This apotheosis involves an intriguing inversion of his usual incarnation as the 'superman' able to perform extraordinary tasks in large part by drawing upon his own extensive resources. Instead, Herakles is given a passivity lacking from his other activities. In the chariot scenes showing his journey to Olympos, he is standing rigidly on the chariot while Athena is holding the reins. It has been observed that the scenes are resonant of depictions of ancient Greek weddings on which the bride would be conveyed to her new home in a chariot driven by the groom. At the time, then, when he is making the transition from human to god, he temporarily takes on a degree of passivity redolent of the quintessentially passive figure in iconographical terms: the bride.

If Herakles is the bride, Athena is, effectively, the bridegroom. The striking nature of the inversion has not been lost on commentators (e.g. Leduc 1996) who have noted the incongruity between Athena, the virgin *par excellence*, adopting a characteristic male role and Herakles, the great deflowerer of women, being depicted as her bride. The use of wedding imagery is discernible, too, in Athena's introduction of Herakles to Zeus. Figure 6 presents a comparable image of feminine passivity on the part of Herakles as set against masculine dominance of Athena. Athena is leading, if not pulling, Herakles towards Zeus by holding him by the wrist. This action evokes one of the standard features of wedding iconography, the *cheir epi karpō* ('hand on wrist') gesture whereby, in a movement with connotations of abduction, the seemingly unwilling bride was led to her destination.

The unique closeness of Athena and Herakles is also depicted on several intimate scenes on Greek vases (for references, see Deacy 2005: 40–1). In some of these scenes the two figures are shown resting with one another or else engaging in recreational activities. Athena is often shown standing beside Herakles while he is reclining. In other scenes he is playing the lyre while Athena is at his side. Elsewhere, Athena is given the role of his cup-bearer in that she is pouring from a jug into a vessel that he is holding out. Other vase paintings show them performing a handshake. Attempting an interpretation of these scenes is a frustrating process because it is unclear where we should place them in Herakles' myth. Is Athena keeping him company while he takes a break from his labours? Should they alternatively be viewed as post-apotheosis scenes depicting two deities taking pleasure in one another's company? Whichever is the case, they portray an intimacy and personal bond that exceeds any other of Athena's relationships, even that with her father Zeus.

'THE ZEUS-BORN TROJAN GIRL'

Athena has emerged in this chapter as the goddess capable of bringing about surprising, and seemingly impossible, outcomes to various situations. Her interventions in the Trojan War provide perhaps the most extreme instance of this ability. The well-being of Troy ought to have been guaranteed. Not only were the Trojans more dear to Zeus than any other people (e.g. *Iliad* 4.44–9), but the city was under the protection of Athena herself thanks to its possession of the palladion, the statue of Athena believed to have talisman-like properties. Situated in her temple on the peak of the akropolis of Troy, it was supposed to convey special protective powers, possibly due to the belief that Athena herself had created the image in the likeness of her dead friend Pallas (see below, this chapter). Thanks to the actions of Athena, however, Troy was ultimately sacked by the Greeks.

The story of Troy is in part the story of the fall from grace of a city under Athena's protection. Paris' choice of Aphrodite's gift in the contest on Mount Ida ensured Athena's antagonism towards the Trojans. Athena is, after all, in the words of Iolaos quoted at the head of this chapter, the goddess 'who will not put up with defeat'. So begins one of the most poignant themes of the Trojan myth, the Trojans' lack of awareness that that they have permanently lost Athena's patronage. In *Iliad* 6, for example, the women seek her protection against Diomedes while he is ranging through the battlefield:

> Going into the great house, she [Hekabe] called out to her handmaidens, who assembled throughout the city the highborn women; while she descended into the fragrant store-chamber. There lay the elaborately wrought robes, the work of Sidonian women, whom Paris himself, the godlike, had brought home from the land of Sidon, crossing the wide sea, on that journey when he brought back also gloriously descended Helen. Hekabe lifted out one and took it as gift to Athena, that which was loveliest in design and the largest, and shone like a star. It lay beneath the others. She went on her way, and a throng of noble women hastened about her. When these had come to Athena's temple on the peak of the citadel, Theano of the fair cheeks opened the door for them . . . she whom

the Trojans had established to be Athena's priestess. With a wailing cry all lifted up their hands to Athena, and Theano of the fair cheeks taking up the robe laid it along the knees of Athena the lovely haired, and praying she supplicated the daughter of great Zeus: 'O lady, Athena, our city's defender, shining among goddesses, break the spear of Diomedes, and grant that the man be hurled on his face in front of the Skaian gates; so may we instantly dedicate within your shrine twelve heifers, yearlings, never broken, if only you will have pity on the town of Troy, and the Trojan wives, and their innocent children.'

(286–310, Lattimore translation, very slightly adapted)

Athena's rejection of the prayer is recounted in a single line:

So she spoke in prayer, but Pallas Athena threw her head back.

(311)

The practice of Greek religion normally involved the establishment of a bond between the worshipper, who performed the appropriate rituals, and the deity whose good favour could be secured though prayers and offerings. Athena refuses to 'play the game' as it were, turning aside her head rather than granting her favours. When her favourites require her assistance she is the 'goddess of nearness' whose interventions help bring about their success, but she is just as capable of rejecting a request even one performed, as here, in the appropriate ritual location and led by the designated priestess. The 'goddess of nearness' is also in some contexts an implacable deity, bearing out the characterisation of her in the *Homeric Hymns* as 'possessing an unbending heart' (28.2).

We saw above that Athena helps her friends. She harms her enemies too. This aspect of her operation as a deity is strikingly apparent in the duel between Achilleus and Hektor recounted in *Iliad* 22 that culminates in the death of the Trojan hero. When the contest had reached a stalemate, with Hektor running around the city walls chased by Achilleus who was unable to catch him, Athena appeared before Hektor disguised as his brother Deiphobos, persuading him to stand his ground with his brother's assistance. The fight resumes and Hektor finds himself alone, having been cheated by Athena:

> Lifting his voice he called aloud on Deiphobos of the pale shield, and asked him
> for a long spear, but Deiphobos was not near him. And Hektor knew the truth
> inside his heart, and spoke aloud: 'No use. Here at last the gods have sum-
> moned me deathward. I thought Deiphobos the hero was here close beside me,
> but he is behind the wall and it was Athena cheating me, and now evil death is
> close to me.'
>
> (293–300, Lattimore translation, very slightly adapted)

This incident demonstrates the lengths to which the goddess was considered to be willing to go to attain her ends. It is not enough in this instance that she should assist one of her favourites. In order to engineer his success, she deceives his enemy too. Heroic warfare is frequently presented as unpleasant; Athena is assigned an unpleasantness to match.

Although the *Iliad* does not recount the fall of Troy, the ultimate fate of the city is an underlying theme of the epic. In a sense, Athena's role in breaking the stalemate between Hektor and Achilleus points ahead to her resolution of a further seemingly impossible problem: how to take the city. After ten years of attempting to penetrate the walls through military prowess, the Greeks finally entered the city via an act of cunning. Having led the Trojans to believe that they were abandoning the War and sailing for home, they presented to them the giant wooden horse, an apparent gift to Athena in her guise as 'the Zeus-born Trojan girl' (Euripides, *Trojan Women* 526), but that was actually fashioned under Athena's instruction.

Thanks to the stratagem of Athena, the Greeks were able to penetrate the city. It was while they were sacking it that the act was committed that ensured that, like the Trojans before them, they lost her patronage. The Trojan princess Kassandra had taken refuge at the palladion but was dragged away from it by Ajax the son of Oileus. Athena's anger was generated not by the act *per se*, but by the failure on the part of the Greeks to punish the violator. When Agamemnon made a last-ditch attempt to 'accomplish holy hecatombs so as to soften Athena's deadly anger' (Homer, *Odyssey* 3.114–15, Lattimore translation slightly adapted), he is labelled by the narrator a 'poor fool' thanks to his lack of awareness 'that she would not listen to him' (145–6). Her protection replaced with animosity, he had no more chance of successfully propitiating her than did the Trojan women in *Iliad* 6. Not only does she withhold her protection but she actively intervenes in order to create the storm on Cape Kaphereos that destroyed most of the fleet (e.g. Alkaios *fr.* 298).

MYTHIC FEMALES: HELPING MEN, HARMING WOMEN

As the helper of heroes, Athena functions almost as a kind of 'big sister' figure, watching out for her favourites and supporting them selflessly. As we shall now consider, women of myth often come to grief when they come into contact with her. Arachne, the wool-worker famed for her weaving, is turned by her into a spider for challenging the goddess to a contest (Chapter 3). Another skilled female, a girl called Murmix, was transformed into an ant when she attempted to claim credit for one of Athena's inventions, the plough (Servius, *On Virgil's Aeneid* 4.402). Another young woman, Medusa, suffers the most grotesque of transformations at Athena's hands. Originally a beautiful young woman, Athena turned her into the epitome of ugliness when, according to one version of her story, she had sex with Poseidon in Athena's temple (Ovid, *Metamorphoses* 4.794–803; 6.119–20).

Athena's childhood friend, a girl called Pallas, even dies at her hands. After her birth, according to Apollodoros (3.12.3), Zeus placed her in the tutelage of the river god Triton, who raised her alongside his own daughter. One day, the girls were training in the arts of war when things turned nasty. When Pallas was about to strike Athena, Zeus, who was observing the girls at play, interposed the aegis. While Pallas was startled by this apparition, Athena accidentally struck a fatal blow. What the story illustrates is that females who come into contact with Athena are rarely fated to thrive. Athena is a powerful female, but she is not – in myth – a woman's goddess.

While some women do benefit from Athena's assistance, they do so as 'by-products' of Athena's patronage of the men in their lives.

Odysseus' wife Penelope, for example, is aided by the goddess in her attempts to ward off the suitors. More often, women in heroic myths suffer due to Athena's interventions on behalf of heroes. The Troizenian princess Aithra, for example, was the victim of the goddess' powers to deceive. Athena appeared to her in a dream telling her to go to the island of Sphairia to perform a libation. It was there that Aithra was raped by Poseidon and impregnated with Theseus (Pausanias 2.33.1).

Athena is at home in the world of men. Virgin young woman though she is, she forms close attachments with a range of heroes. When she comes into contact with females, the consequences tend not to be favourable for the women in question. This further confirms our characterisation of Athena as a 'Mrs Thatcher' figure, the female who supports her male protégés but whose status as a strong female does not make her a friend to women. Her relations with mythic females bring suffering or death to the women in question: women who are in various respects similar to herself: workers, parthenoi and, in one instance, a young warrior. In the 'real world', Athena was the patron of woolworking. In her mythic roles, she was not a woman's goddess.

OVERVIEW

Athena was the greatest friend that a hero could have. She intervenes on behalf of a range of heroes to help them attain success in their various endeavours. Each time, the kind of help that she provides is ideally suited to the hero in question and to the particular circumstances in which he finds himself. At times, she provides a useful gift, equipping Perseus, for example, with the various tools required to acquire the head of the Gorgon. Heroes still have to work hard to attain their goals. Far from limiting their heroism (Ajax's misunderstanding), she provides a divine dimension to their achievements while inspiring them and enabling them to realise their potential as heroes.

With Athena on the side of a hero, he could not fail in his endeavours. Conversely, with Athena as an enemy, an individual or a group could not succeed. As well as a dedicated champion, as an enemy she was at once unforgiving and implacable. Once dishonoured by the Trojans, she worked against them, using her powers to promote the Greeks and undermine the Trojans. But Athena's patronage was not something to be taken for granted, as may be demonstrated by her response to Lesser Ajax's desecration of her sanctuary during the sack of Troy.

Athena's interventions in the lives of heroes show her to be willing to come among mortals to assist them in their endeavours. She is a goddess at home on Olympos, and on earth too. The following chapters will investigate another aspect of her 'nearness', her role as the patron of cities.

5

ATHENA IN ATHENS: PATRON, SYMBOL AND 'MOTHER'

Both the city and all the land are alike sacred to Athena, for even those who in the demes have an established worship of other gods nevertheless hold Athena in honour.

(Pausanias 1.26.6, Loeb translation slightly adapted)

INTRODUCTION

One of the best-known aspects of Athena is her connection with Athens. Her sanctuary on the north side of the Akropolis summit was the home of the city's principal cult, whose sacred image, a formless piece of olive-wood believed variously to have fallen from the sky or to have been erected by the hero Erichthonios, is the only divine statue known to have been taken away for safekeeping prior to invasion by the Persians in 480 BC. Athena was the 'great-hearted goddess' in the words of Solon (fragment 4, see below), who ensured the well-being of the land, its people and their institutions. The question of which came first – the name of the city or the name of the goddess – has long vexed scholars (Burkert 1985: 139), but the degree of pride produced by the linguistic affiliation of Athena–Athens may be demonstrated by Athenian coins, which in addition to depicting a helmeted head of Athena and two of her local attributes – the owl and the olive branch – contained the inscription ATE, the first three letters of both goddess and city.

Figure 7 Athenian tetradrachm, c. 490 BC; first published in *Nordisk familjebok* (1904–1926).

The special place accorded to Athena is something that requires an explanation, especially when we take account of the fact that while placing particular emphasis upon Athena, the Athenians worshipped literally hundreds of divine beings. The city was, in fact, renowned in the ancient world for the extraordinary size of its pantheon. On his visit, St Paul, for one, found himself in a city 'over-run with idols' (*Acts* 17.16). We will explore the ways in which the Athenians at once paid special attention to Athena while situating her within their pantheon. For one thing, as we shall see, they presented her as versatile goddess, with characteristics that overlapped with those more commonly linked with two of her fellow deities, Zeus and Aphrodite.

The main focus of this chapter will be the conditions that were in place in Athens that enabled her to have such predominance in the religious system of the city. How these developed is not a concern for us here: we will tackle this contentious question in the next chapter. This chapter will look at how, in the archaic and classical periods, aspects of her divinity were understood. We shall begin with an investigation of her relationship with Zeus, the main god of the Olympian pantheon and also, of course, her father. Then we will examine how the Athenians thought she had become their patron goddess: through vying with Poseidon for the land. Finally, and in the most detail, we will examine her role in the story of Erichthonios, the foundation myth of the Athenian citizenry.

This chapter deals with important issues in its own right while serving as an extended introduction to issues to be explored in the following two chapters, which will adopt a largely chronological approach to Athena's cult in Athens. One aim is to demonstrate why Athena was so appealing an image by thinking about what it was that made people venerate her. In particular, we will look at her role as a unifier, who provided a focus for expressions of Athenian identity. We will also begin in this chapter to address the question of her gendered identity in Athenian myth and cult. Athens is renowned as the patriarchal city *par excellence*, whose political system relegated women to a marginal status and denied them any part in the running of the city. The women of Athens are typically viewed as oppressed, restricted largely to the women's quarters and with limited opportunities for communal gathering. We will begin exploring the nature of Athena's femininity in an attempt to recover how far notions of the feminine and of women's place in society impacted upon perceptions and representations. How far, for example, did the Athenians downplay her femininity? In what ways did they regard it as crucial to her divine nature?

ATHENA, ZEUS AND SOCIAL COHESION

Among the many levels at which Greek religion operated, the Olympian and the local were two of the most significant. The gods worshipped in particular poleis were, in part, localised versions of their Olympian guises. It was at the interplay of local and pan-hellenic that divine characteristics and roles were largely produced. In Athens, Athena was the major deity, with a centrality that exceeded that of any other local tutelary god. At the Olympian level, meanwhile, she was one of the many inferiors of Zeus, albeit with a special relationship with him as his daughter and enforcer. This section will investigate what this local/panhellenic disjunction tells us about local perceptions of Athena and Zeus.

Zeus had a major role in the religious life of the city, with key festivals including the Diasia, the Dipolieia and the Olympieia. But, widely worshipped though he was, his cult lacked the centrality that is evident elsewhere in the Greek world (Dowden 2006: 65). This imbalance between his panhellenic and local status might have been removed, as Dowden suggests (2006: 77), had the Peisistratid tyranny (see figure 11) endured past 510 BC. One of the projects begun by the tyrants was a huge temple of Zeus Olympios on a ridge to the southeast of the Akropolis. It was left incomplete after the fall of the tyranny, however, and finally finished off only centuries later, under Hadrian. It is possible that with a grand temple in his honour, Zeus's cult would have posed a challenge to the centrality of Athena's. As it was, however, Athena's ascendancy remained unchallenged.

One of Zeus's principal roles throughout Greece was as the promoter of cohesion and social unity, in which guise he was envisaged as presiding over a range of gatherings at city and tribal levels. There was a panhellenic dimension to this role via his role as the god of Olympia, where representatives of the poleis gathered quadrennially for a celebration of *to hellenikon* ('Greekness'). In Athens, Athena's cult appears to have provided the unifying focus that elsewhere came under the remit of Zeus. The major festival in her honour, the Panathenaia, provided an opportunity for the whole of the population to gather together in a show of unity, honouring the goddess and also honouring themselves as a collective group (see further, Chapter 6).

But at the same time, the Athenians were able to link the local pre-eminence of Athena with the Olympian religious dimension by stressing the mythic relationship between her and Zeus. Her birth was one of the most popular and most widely represented myths in the archaic and classical city. A popular scene on vase paintings (see e.g. figures 1 and 2), it was the subject, too, of the eastern pediment of the Parthenon (Chapter 7). In celebrating Athena at the Panathenaia, the Athenians were effectively honouring Zeus too, given that the central day of the festival, Hekatombaion 28, was the day of her birth. The festival also celebrated another myth which linked Athena and Zeus, the gigantomachy. It was this myth that was represented on the peplos presented to the olivewood image of Athena. This, the holiest object given to Athena each year, celebrated how she fought alongside her father in support of his regime.

In celebrating Athena, the Athenians repeatedly evoked her relationship with Zeus. This is something that may be exemplified further in the first ever reference to the goddess by an Athenian author, the poet/politician Solon. Solon was outlining the situation facing him as a reformer in the early sixth century BC, when civil strife had taken Athens to crisis point. But while conflict among citizens is producing suffering, he states, the city is protected from unfriendly divine intervention because of the willingness of Athena to intercede on her people's behalf:

> Our city will never be destroyed by the pronouncement of Zeus, nor by the wish of the blessed immortal gods for such is she, our great hearted goddess, mightily fathered [*obrimopatrē*], who protects us, Pallas Athena, who holds out her hands over us.

(fr. 4.1–4)

One of the ideas connected with Athena we saw in Chapter 4, that, with the goddess on side, success could be guaranteed, is given a local twist in this poem. It also alludes to another aspect of the goddess, namely that her effectiveness as a deity derives from her privileged status as daughter of Zeus, producing a pecking order (cf. Herington 1963: 63) of:

Zeus
↓
Athena
↓
Athens

Athena's pre-eminence in the local pantheon is emphasised. So too is her place under the overall authority of Zeus.

The relationship between Athena and Zeus operates at two levels. As the chief Olympian, Zeus is the supreme god of the Greek pantheon. Athena, meanwhile, was the pre-eminent deity of Athens but with her status as daughter of Zeus strengthening her credentials as tutelary deity.

In other ways too, Athena and Zeus were linked in Athenian cult. While sacred above all to Athena Polias, the Akropolis was also the home of Zeus Polieus, whose sanctuary was situated to the northeast of the Parthenon. The sacred olive trees (*moriai*) of Attica, the descendants of the original tree that secured Athena's patronage (see below, this chapter) were sacred both to Zeus Morios and Athena Moria. The gods were also jointly evoked as the founders of the city, Zeus Archegetis and Athena Archegetes. Another festival of Zeus, the Diisoteria included procession to Zeus Soter ('saviour') and Athena Soteria. In various specialist guises, the two gods presided over a range of civic institutions. The Boule (Council), for example, was sacred to Zeus Boulaios and Athena Boulaia, while the patron gods of the phratries were Zeus Phratrios and Athena Phratria.

Zeus and Athena were cult partners whose powers could be jointly evoked in various contexts. This shows us once again that Athena's local pre-eminence did not preclude the veneration of other deities. With this in mind, we will move to the myth of how Athena became patron of Athens. This will enable us to deal with the relationship between Athena and another Greek deity, Poseidon, whereby Athena was presented as the superior in the local pantheon while the power of her fellow god was duly acknowledged too.

POSEIDON AND THE CONTEST FOR THE LAND

Various ancient Greek peoples claimed a special relationship with Athena by regarding her as native to their city or region. As far as the Boiotians seem to have been concerned, for example, she was born beside a 'small torrent' (Pausanias 9.33.7) called the Triton which ran through the Alalkomeneion, one of her major sanctuaries in the region. In Arcadia, meanwhile, her birthplace was said to be the sanctuary of Zeus Lecheatos ('in child bed') in Aliphera (Pausanias 8.26.6). Although the Athenians were the people who claimed an especially close link with the goddess, they did not regard her as indigenous. Instead, they considered her to have been born beside the Libyan Triton, her 'natal stream' (*genethlios poros*) as it is described in Aeschylus' *Eumenides* (293).

Athena's association with the city was instituted by another means, her contest with Poseidon:

> Kekrops, an autochthon, with a body compounded of man and serpent, was the first king of Attica, and the land which was formerly called Akte he named

Kekropia after himself. In his time, they say, the gods resolved to take possession of cities in which each of them should receive his own peculiar worship. So
Poseidon was the first that came to Attica, and with a blow of his trident on the
middle of the Akropolis, he produced a sea which they now call Erechtheis. After
him came Athena, and, having called on Kekrops to witness her act of taking
possession, she planted an olive tree, which is still shown in the Pandroseion.
But when the two struggled for possession of the country, Zeus parted them
and appointed arbiters, not, as some have affirmed, Kekrops and Kranaos, nor
yet Erysichthon, but the twelve gods. And in accordance with their verdict
the country was awarded to Athena, because Kekrops bore witness that she had
been the first to plant the olive. Athena, therefore, called the city Athens after
herself, and Poseidon in hot anger flooded the Thriasian plain and laid Attica
under the sea.

(3.14.1, Loeb translation, adapted)

The opposition between Athena and Poseidon that we investigated
earlier in this book (Chapter 3) is adapted to the local circumstances
at Athens as they vie for supremacy, with the olive-giver, Athena,
contrasted to Poseidon the elemental power who makes a 'sea'
appear on the Akropolis summit. Athena is the bringer of civilisation, who creates the city's staple crop. After her victory, she per-
forms a further civilising act: that of name giving. Poseidon, in
contrast, lives up to his nature as the elemental power of the sea,
sending a flood in his 'hot anger'. The myth expressed for the
Athenians both why Poseidon merited worship as a powerful
potentially dangerous deity and why Athena was better suited
to the tutelary role as the provider of the gift more useful to the
nascent city.

ATHENA'S 'CHILDREN': THE STORY OF THE
BIRTH OF ERICHTHONIOS

As well as dealing with Athena's emergence as patron deity, local
myth also explained how she came to be involved in the myth of the
origins of the citizen body. The story in question brings her into
connection with another major local deity, Hephaistos, with whom

she is responsible for the production of the miracle child, Erichthonios, sometimes known also as Erechtheus (see Chapter 6). He was the ancestor of the Athenian citizenry, a hero who was both 'Very-of-the-Earth' (*Eri-chthonios*, an alternative understanding of his name from Erion-chthonios [p. 53 above]) and the offspring of two of the city's major deities. As we saw above (Chapter 3), Athena went to Hephaistos because she wanted him to make weapons for her. However, as he had been rejected by Aphrodite, he became sexually attracted to Athena and began to pursue her for sex. As we would expect of a warrior virgin, Athena rejected his advances, although she did not stand her ground but fled. Though he is lame, a point stressed in the Apollodoros account quoted earlier in Chapter 3, he managed to catch up with her. He then attempted to rape her, but she fought him off, although in one of the most extraordinary instances of anthropomorphism in Greek myth, he did manage to ejaculate over her leg. Athena, 'in disgust' according to Apollodoros, wiped off the semen with a piece of wool and cast it to the ground. When it hit the ground, Erichthonios was born. The story as narrated by Apollodoros continues as follows, providing a convenient summary of other accounts:

> Athena raised him unknown to the other gods because she wanted to make him immortal, and she put him in a chest and committed it to Pandrosos, daughter of Kekrops, forbidding her to open it. But Pandrosos' sisters opened the chest in their curiosity and saw a serpent coiled about the infant. As some would have it, they were killed by the snake, while others said that Athena's anger drove them mad, and they threw themselves from the Akropolis. Erichthonios was raised by Athena herself in the sacred precinct.
>
> (3.14.6)

In this section, we will examine various ideas about Athena presented in the myth: how she is gendered and her role as the potential provider of immortality. The myth's aetiological aspects will then be explored, including how the myth accounts for Athena's relationship with Hephaistos and with other divine beings of the local pantheon. We will end by examining the potential role of the myth as an aetion for the Arrhephoria, one of the most intriguing of the local rituals performed in the city.

Gendering Athena

The myth is perhaps the most inventive local account about any of the major Greek gods, not least because of the range of images of mythic femininity that are adduced in relation to Athena. She is present in her characteristic guise of the warrior virgin, who desires to equip herself with weapons and who is eager to maintain her virginity at any cost. There are intriguing similarities, too, between Athena and a type of young woman who regularly appears in Greek myth, the parthenos ('young woman of marriageable age') who falls prey to the sexual attentions of a god and flees from him only to be caught, deflowered and impregnated (Deacy 1997a). It has become usual to envisage Athena as some sort of androgynous or sexless figure (e.g. Just 1989: 278–9), 'a bit of a stiff' as a fellow academic once described her to me. This story presents us with a rather different image of Athena. She is constructed as a nubile and sexually attractive female, comparable in part to other young women of myth who attract the attention of a god, are subjected to sexual assault and produce a child.

This is not all. As well as drawing on myths of divine rape, the story depicts Athena in a manner that is resonant of the sex-goddess Aphrodite, the 'official' wife of Hephaistos among the Olympians, who would more usually be contrasted to the virgin Athena. In Apollodoros' account, as we saw, Hephaistos attempted to have sex with Athena after he had been rejected by Aphrodite. In effect, Erichthonios becomes the 'child' of Athena because the goddesses have temporarily swapped roles, with Aphrodite having rejected sex and Athena becoming sexually attractive. Athena is accorded characteristics normally alien to her, those of a nubile, attractive female, just long enough to involve her in the conception of Erichthonios.

And so an impossibility occurs, a kind of Greek precursor to the Virgin Birth. Visual depictions show Ge emerging out of the ground handing the child over to Athena. Athena is reaching out to take the baby; the child is, in turn, reaching out to her. A touching, intimate scene, this even evokes depictions on vases of servants handing over children to their mothers. In some of the images, such as figure 8,

Figure 8 Athena receives Erichthonios from Ge, Attic red-figure cup, Berlin, Antikenmuseum 2537; redrawn by S.J. Deacy.

a red-figure bowl by the Kodros Painter from around 440 BC, Athena is wearing the aegis, but it is round the back, at once enabling her to receive the child, and, presumably, to ensure that it will not frighten him.

The representation of Athena in this myth is far removed from the image of the warrior female whose power derives from her weapons. In perhaps the most striking departure from usual depictions, Athena has a downward gaze very different from her usual penetrating stare with its power to disarm and dazzle. We are presented, instead, with a more 'proper' image of woman-hood: a modest, even demure gaze more suited to the 'doe-eyed' (*bo-opis*) Hera.

Mortality and immortality

Once Erichthonios was born, Athena, as set out in Apollodoros' account, wanted to give the child the ultimate gift a deity might bestow upon a favourite: immortality. She placed him in a chest which she entrusted to the daughters of Kekrops, Pandrosos and two girls not named by Apollodoros: Aglauros and Herse. As is the way when mythic figures are told not to look in a chest, curiosity got the better of two of the girls. As Euripides' *Ion* puts it in a conversa-tion between two of the play's characters:

> ION: I heard that the young girls opened the goddess' chest.
> KREOUSA: And so they died, staining the rocks of the Akropolis with their
>   blood.
>
> (273–4)

Once interrupted, the immortalisation process was spoiled. Quite why this should have been the case is not clear although the situation has a parallel in another foiled immortalisation attempt. As narrated in the *Homeric Hymn to Demeter* (235ff.), Demeter, dis-guised as an old woman, had been gradually making the Eleusinian child, Demophoön, immortal, in this instance by sticking him into fire at night, when she was alone with the child. The process was ruined when, one night, someone else observed what was going on: the child's mother Metaneira.

Athena (like Demeter in the *Hymn*) was furious. Sources other than Apollodoros narrate that she happened to be carrying a boulder to fortify the Akropolis when informed by the crow what had taken place. In her anger, she dropped the rock, and the result was the prominent but strategically useless Mount Lykabettos. As for the crow, it was banned from the Akropolis. Her anger was not vented at Erichthonios, which enables us to contrast the story to another account of foiled immortality, that of Tydeus, whose own actions (Chapter 4) led Athena to withdraw the gift. Here instead, Athena cares for the child, bringing him up in her sanctuary. Athena becomes the nurturer of the hero, with a closeness to him that has a maternal dimension even if she is not biologically his mother. The goddess who was envisaged by Solon as the one who 'holds out her hands' over the people, was envisaged in mythological terms as having this relationship from the time when she nourished the ancestral hero.

Myth and cult

The Athenian Akropolis was packed with cult sites, especially on the north side of the summit and along the slopes. One of the roles of the myth was to establish a relationship between the cult of Athena and other cult artefacts and beings. It is on the Akropolis that the child is placed in his chest. It is from the rock too that the girls hurl themselves to their death. When the plan to make him immortal is thwarted, Erichthonios is raised in the sacred precinct, presumably the temple of Athena Polias. The myth also deals with the development of Athena's cult in that Erichthonios was said to be responsible for the erection of her statue and for the establishment of the Panathenaia. As for other characters in the myth, they also have connections with the Athenian cult. The altar of Hephaistos was one of a cluster of holy objects on the north side of the summit. Pandrosos, the obedient daughter, was worshipped in a precinct on the north side of the summit, while Aglauros had a sanctuary

Figure 9 The Akropolis summit, with the Erechtheion to the left and the Parthenon to the right. Mount Lykabettos is visible in the distance, to the right of the Erechtheion; photo: Daniel Dench.

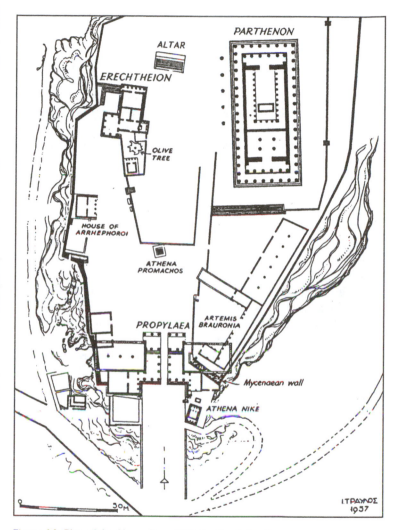

Figure 10 Plan of the Akropolis c. 400 BC; after J. Travlos.

on one of the slopes, as befits a girl who died when she threw herself off the rock. Aphrodite was the goddess who, after Athena, had the strongest connections to the Akropolis thanks to her many sanctuaries on its slopes (Rosenzweig 2004: esp. chs 2, 3, 6).

The myth takes on a further level of significance when we have a brief look at one of the statues that we will examine in detail in two chapters' time, the Athena Parthenos of Pheidias (figure 15), which shows Athena with an attribute, a serpent. This is presumably the guardian serpent of the Akropolis, a being who was thought to inhabit a crevice in the north side of the summit. Its connection both with the well-being of the Akropolis and with the goddess emerges from a story in Herodotos concerning how, on the eve of the Persian invasion of 480, it reportedly failed to eat the honey cake that was provided for it each month, an occurrence that was, Herodotos states, taken as a sign that Athena herself had deserted the city (8.41).

Is this serpent is to be identified with Erichthonios? In Apollodoros' account, the girls see him with a serpent coiled around himself, a sign perhaps that he was half way to becoming immortalised when the chest was opened. This is not something that can be established with certainty; serpents are, however, pertinent symbols of immortality because they shed their skins. A connection with serpents and immortality may explain why, in other sources, he is envisaged as, either semi-serpentine in form or even wholly serpentine (Powell 1906). In his description of the Athena Parthenos statue, Pausanias explicitly identifies the serpent as Erichthonios (1.24.5). If this is the case, the myth is not just about Erichthonios as the ancestor nurtured by Athena. It also concerns Erichthonios as the guardian serpent who was nourished with regular food offerings by designated religious personnel.

Among the most intriguing rites for which we possess evidence is the Arrhephoria, a secret, noctural journey made in midsummer by two young girls from the Akropolis to some spot below it, one possibly connected with Aphrodite. These girls, the Arrhephoroi, or 'carriers of sacred things', had spent the year housed on the Akropolis engaging in cult activities. Their year ended in the following way, according to Pausanias:

Two young girls dwell not far from the temple of the Polias, whom the Athenians call Arrhephoroi. For a time, they are lodged with the goddess, but when the festival comes round, they perform by night the following rites. Having put on their heads what the priestess of Athena gives them to carry, although what it is that she gives is known neither her nor by them, the girls descend by the natural underground passage that goes across the adjacent precincts, within the city, of Aphrodite in the Gardens. They leave down below what they carry, and receive back something else which they bring back covered up. These girls they then discharge and take up to the Akropolis others in their place.

(1.27.3)

One problem faced when tackling the evidence is how far Pausanias' account is to be trusted, including as it does several vague details, while leaving much unexplained. What was in the baskets, for example? Who knew what was inside them if the Priestess was kept unaware? What was the girls' destination: the sanctuary of Aphrodite, or some spot near her sanctuary? Responses to the account have ranged from the suggestion that Pausanias was being deliberately vague to protect the secrecy of the rite to the possibility that he did not himself know what went on.

Pausanias' account has served as the starting point for an extensive body of work (see 'further reading' below), much of which has centred upon the parallels between the rite and the Erichthonios story. Both involve two girls, a descent from the summit of the Akropolis and something secret in a chest; both, too, make a connection between Athena and Aphrodite. There are a number of details that do not fit together perfectly, although this need not necessarily be a problem. Where we have links between myths and rituals, it is misleading to look for exact parallels; rather we should think about how each reflects upon comparable communal concerns. In this case, the myth and cult may be providing complementary ways of engaging with the notion of a sexualised Athena, who – to become the mother of the ancestral hero – is brought into association with Aphrodite, her fellow Akropolis goddess. The rite seems to be presenting a further connection between Athena and the Akropolis, extending her links from the summit to the slopes, the home of Aphrodite.

OVERVIEW

What do the myths and cults we have been exploring tell us about Athena? The connection established with the city when she fought with Poseidon to become its patron deity is extended to the citizen body when she became involved in the conception, birth and rearing of Erichthonios. The myths explain Athena's close tie with the Akropolis as the place whose patronage she was willing to vie for with Poseidon and, subsequently, as the place where she raised a child. The Akropolis was a crowded place comprising numerous cults and religious artefacts, but with a unifying figure, Athena, who linked many of them, including various phenomena on the summit such as the olive tree, the salt spring, the altar of Hephaistos and the precinct of Pandrosos, and on the slopes, the sanctuaries of Aglauros and Aphrodite. The connections enable us to engage with the duality expressed at the start of this chapter connected with Athenian religion, its simultaneous veneration of numerous beings and particular elevation of Athena. This was not a contradiction: rather than a deity whose cult was in competition with other beings, she functioned as a kind of common denominator, through whom links were created with particular gods and heroes of the local pantheon.

Far from operating in isolation, Athena had ties with a range of beings, notably her fellow gods Zeus, Demeter, Poseidon, Hephaistos and Aphrodite, and various local heroes and heroines including Erichthonios and Erechtheus, the Kekropids and Praxithea. Athens comes close to being a henotheism, a system where one god was venerated above all others, but she was also a being integrated into the polytheistic system via her ties with other beings. We will move, in Chapters 6 and 7, to a consideration of the Athenians' veneration of Athena from another perspective, a chronological one, to trace how the goddess–polis relationship was expressed at particular points in the history of the city.

As well as the warrior virgin, local myth presented Athena as, variously, a vulnerable young woman and a mother who possesses certain traits more usually associated with her fellow Akropolis goddess, Aphrodite. Our examination has enabled us to begin to

assess the impact of views of femininity upon Athena's representation in Athens. Far from underrating her femininity, a variety of
female models were adduced in order to construct her as a goddess.
The Erichthonios myth presents something 'slippery' about Athena
in gendered terms, attributing to her a range of images, each of
which suits a particular stage of the myth.

EARLY ATHENIAN HISTORY

'Athene the goddess is Athens itself – i.e. the real and concrete spirit of the citizens.'

(Hegel 1956: 252)

INTRODUCTION

In the previous chapter, we looked at the qualities that particularly distinguish Athena as an Athenian deity. She was connected with communality and civic identity while envisaged, too, as being committed to the patronage of the city. There was an almost maternal dimension to that protection expressed in her connection with the ancestral hero, Erichthonios. This chapter will examine these qualities further as we move from a largely thematic account to a more chronological approach. We will begin with the tricky question of the earliest evidence, seeking whether her Akropolis cult can be traced as far back as the Bronze Age. From this we will consider how the goddess' role as protectress of the urban centre came to be extended to the whole of Attica, either in the Dark Ages or in the eighth century BC. We will move to firmer ground as we turn to the sixth and early fifth centuries when we can begin to trace more confidently her worship and perceptions. The role of the state will be examined in the development of her cult, with a particular focus on the tyrant Peisistratos and his promotion of her cult and image.

Period	Selected Political Events	Selected Cultural and Religious Events
Middle Neolithic (c.5000–4000 BC)	Earliest habitation on the Akropolis	
Mycenaean Period (c.1600–1065 BC)	Palace on Akropolis 1259/8? Unification of Attika	
Dark Ages to Geometic period (c.1100–700 BC)	Emergence of the first poleis (c.800–700)	First Temple of Athena Polias (c.750–700)? Second Temple of Athena Polias (c.700–650)?
Archaic period (c.700–479 BC)	Attempted tyranny of Kylon (632/1) Drakon's lawcode (621/0) Solon's reforms (594)	Establishment of sanctuary of Athena Nike (c.575–50) Establishment of Great Panathenaia (566/5) Old Temple of Athena (565–60)
	Peisistratos' first tyranny (561/0?) Peisistratos' second tyranny (557/6?) Peisistratos' third tyranny (546–527) Tyranny of Hippias (527–10) Democratic reforms (508/7) First Persian invasion of Greece; Battle of Marathon (490) Persian Wars (480–79); sack of Athens (480)	Peisistratos' chariot ride with Phye 'Older Parthenon' begun (490–80)
Classical period (479–323 BC)	Formation of Delian League (478) Dominance of Perikles in Athenian politics (c.460–29)	Athena Promachos by Pheidias (465/60–455/50) 'Mourning Athena' (460–50)

Figure 11 Chronological table: the history of Athens. Continued

Period	Selected Political Events	Selected Cultural and Religious Events
Classical period (479–323 BC)— *continued*	Transfer of treasury of Delian League to Athens (454)	'Athena Lemnia' by Pheidias (c.450)
		Akropolis building programme begun (449)
		Parthenon (447–32)
	Peloponnesian War (431–04)	Dedication of Athena Parthenos by Pheidias (438)
		Erechtheion begun (or conceived) (c.435)
		Temple of Athena Nike (c.425–20)
		Erechtheion (421–05)
		Parapet of Athena Nike Temple (415–00)
		Erechtheion completed (406/5)

Figure 11—*continued*

THE 'MISTRESS OF AT(H)ANA' AND THE MYCENAEAN PALACE

A traditionally held view has been that Athena was worshipped on the Akropolis at least as early as the Mycenaean period, when a palace was erected on the summit. Athena, it has been held, was venerated in this period as the guardian of the king. In the Dark Ages that followed the collapse of the Mycenaean kingdoms, Athena's protective power is thought to have been transferred from the king to the people as a whole with the site of the palace being used reconfigured as her sanctuary. 'The god himself took the place of the king', as Victor Ehrenberg memorably expressed it (quoted in de Polignac 1995: 2, tr. Lloyd). All this looks neat as a hypothesis but what it rests on is some patchy, not to mention highly problematic, evidence.

One of the 'Linear B' tablets discovered in the Bronze Age palace at Knossos on Krete dating from *c.* 1400 BC lists several deities, some of whom may well be early manifestations of some of the gods worshipped by later Greeks. One of these gods is A-ta-na-po-ti-ni-ja, 'the powerful female goddess of the place At(h)ana'. The tablet has been hailed as evidence for a Bronze Age cult of Athena in Athens, not least as Athena herself appears as Potnia Athenaia or Potni' Athana ('Mistress Athena', or more precisely 'Athena, she who Masters') in later sources (e.g. Hesiod, *Theogony* 966). However, we need to be wary. The tablet does not explicitly call the goddess Athena, but rather the goddess of a place called Athana. It cannot even be said with certainty that this Athana is consonant with Athens.

Other possible evidence for an early Akropolis cult is provided by the Homeric poems, where Athena is referred to twice in relation to Athens, once in the *Iliad* and once in the *Odyssey*. In the *Iliad*, the Athenians are described as:

> The people of great-hearted Erechtheus, whom Athena daughter of Zeus tended, and whom the grain-giving earth bore. Athena set him down in Athens, in her own rich temple, where the sons of the Athenians propitiate her [*or him*] with bulls and lambs as the seasons come around.
>
> (2.546–51)

The *Odyssey* meanwhile relates how:

> Glaukopis Athena . . . came to Marathon and broad-streeted Athens and went into the well-built house of Erechtheus.
>
> (7.77–80)

The problem is that the usefulness of the Homeric poems as evidence for early Greek history and religion is a matter of debate. They were in likelihood composed over many centuries with different periods leaving their mark. The best way to understand them in historical terms is as a kind of melange made up of some elements of the Mycenaean past and certain Dark Age elements. Added to this, some elements from the eighth century BC appear to have found their way into the poems, this being the period when it is usually held that the poems were being written down. In addition, and to compound matters further, certain elements may be as late as the sixth century when, under the Peisistratid tyranny, the epics may have taken on their final form.

An intriguing difference between the two passages is that in the *Iliad* Athena is said to have placed Erechtheus in 'her own rich temple', while the situation is reversed in the *Odyssey* in that the goddess is instead entering Erechtheus' 'well-built house'. A solution to this difference, it has been conjectured, is to read them as evidence for two distinctive stages in the development of the Athenian cult. The *Odyssey* passage is considered to preserve Athena's role in the Mycenaean city, with the mention of her entering Erechtheus' house preserving her role as the guardian of the palace. The *Iliad* passage, meanwhile, would be regarded as preserving one of the eighth-century elements to have found their way into the epics.

This period was one of radical change in the Greek world. The concept of sacred space was being redefined with sanctuaries coming into existence, possibly for the first time, in the second half of the century. The model put forward by François de Polignac in the 1980s (English tr. 1995) has come in for criticism from scholars who take issue with the notion that the concept of sanctuaries was entirely new (Sourvinou-Inwood 1993). But in any case, something new was happening at this time, with a widespread notion for the first time that space should be set aside exclusively for worship. Could it be that Athena's 'rich temple' was one of the products of the eighth-century religious revolution? If so, the construction of Athena's sanctuary on the Akropolis would form part of the wider pattern of sanctuary construction in the Greek world at this time.

But we need to tread with caution. It is necessary to raise the question of whether the passages in fact tell us anything about Athena in Athens prior to the archaic period. It has been mooted that they are Peisistratid interpolations, created in order to write

Athens into the epics and get round the disjunction between the city's cultural dominance in the sixth century and its otherwise minor role in the poems. Another function of the passages might, on this interpretation, have been to help legitimise the tyranny by giving Homeric credentials to cults being promoted under the tyrants. This point is particularly worth bearing in mind in the light of the possible importance of Erechtheus/Erichthonios for Peisistratos, which we will consider below.

THE SYNOECISM

We move to firmer, if still chronologically contentious, ground when we consider how it was that Athena was able to become patron not just of the urban centre but of the whole of Attica. At some point in the early history of Athens an event occurred that provided the conditions for the transformation of Athena's cult to take place. This was the synoecism or unification of Attica, an event variously dated to the late Bronze Age and the early eighth century BC, which saw the towns of Attica made into a single political unit under the control of Athens. As well as ensuring that Athens became the predominant political power in the newly constructed 'monocentric' state, the synoecism gave a centrality to the worship of Athena that was exceptional in the Greek world. Her sanctuary on the Akropolis became the principal cult of the unified state, so that while the various communities continued to possess distinctive festivals and sanctuaries, her patronage was extended to the whole of Attica. So came into being the situation set out by Pausanias as quoted at the head of the previous chapter whereby the urban centre and territory alike were considered to be sacred to Athena.

Pausanias was expressing something exceptional in polis religion. Most cities, were 'bipolar' in terms of their sacred geography, in that their major sanctuaries tended to be situated not on akropoleis but some distance from the urban centre. The most famous non-urban sanctuary, for example, the Argive Heraion was situated around eight kilometres from Argos on a foothill on the edge of the plain of Argos. This would have made it accessible for worship, but not for daily religious activity. Located on a foothill, it would have been visible, too, from some distance away. In the case of Athens, however, we are faced with a major cult that had a visibility unique in the Greek world, combined with an accessibility denied to other major polis gods. With the synoecism, it is likely that we have the origins of the special bond between the goddess and her people.

566 AND ALL THAT: THE SIXTH CENTURY

The year 566 BC saw a development that further transformed the cult of Athena and the Athenians' view of themselves as a religious community. This was the establishment of the Great Panathenaia, an innovation generally attributed to Peisistratos, who, several years later, would embark on the first of his three periods as tyrant of Athens. Establishing just how radical the development would have been is made difficult by a lack of evidence for what the Panathenaia was like prior to 566. It would have been a smaller-scale event, certainly, to mark the goddess' birthday, Hekatombaion 28, and provide the olivewood statue with a new peplos. After 566, the Athenians gathered every four years for a grander celebration of Athena and of themselves as a worshipping group that lasted over several days in Hekatombaion.

The Greeks loved to gather together in mass celebrations of their gods. The Great Panathenaia was splendid even by these standards. It brought together the city's inhabitants in a grand procession comprising various groups of the population – men, women, children, metics, even freed slaves – that wound its way through the city along the Panathenaic Way and up the slopes of the Akropolis. Having reached the Akropolis summit, the procession made its way to the altar of Athena Polias, for a hekatomb (whence the name of the month): a sacrifice of at least one hundred cattle. It was also a sporting and cultural event for competitors from all over the Greek world with events including boxing, wrestling, chariot races, a regatta and a male beauty pageant. There were also competitions for aulos and kithara players and recitations of the Homeric poems. The establishment of the festival demonstrates the emerging confidence of archaic Athens and the appeal of the goddess as its patron. Athens/Athena had acquired a festival able to hold its own among the existing quadrennial festivals of the Greek world, the likes of the Olympic and Pythian Games. In effect, the establishment of the Great Panathenaia elevated Athena Polias to a status worthy of the major panhellenic gods such as Zeus of Olympia and Apollo of Delphi.

Why Peisistratos – if it was he – introduced the Great Panathenaia, is not known, but what emerges from an examination of his rule is the special relationship he seems to have cultivated with Athena. Peisistratos is a politician characterised in one of the main sources for his rule, Herodotos, for his ability to deceive and manipulate the Athenians. This talent for trickery is demonstrated in the means whereby he emerged for the first time as tyrant, in around 560. According to Herodotos, he wounded himself and his mules and came into the Agora demanding a bodyguard. With this bodyguard, he seized the Akropolis and declared himself tyrant (1.59). When, a few years later, his enemies united to oust him, he made an alliance with one of his rivals, Megakles, and devised an even more daring scheme to return to power:

> To bring about his return to power, they devised between them what seems to me the silliest trick which history has to record. The Greeks have never been simpletons; for centuries past they have been distinguished from other nations by superior wits; and of all the Greeks the Athenians are allowed to be the most intelligent: yet it was at the Athenians' expense that this ridiculous trick was played. In the village of Paiania, there was a handsome woman called Phye, nearly six feet tall, whom they fitted out in a suit of armour and mounted in a chariot. Then, after getting her to pose in the most striking attitude, they drove into Athens, where messengers who had preceded them were already, according to their instructions, talking to the people and urging them to welcome Peisistratos back, because the goddess Athena herself had shown him extraordinary honour and was bringing him back to her own Akropolis. They spread this nonsense all over the town, and it was not long before rumours reached the outlying villages. Believing that the woman was the goddess herself, the citizens worshipped her, and welcomed Peisistratos back.

> (1.60, Penguin translation by de Selincourt, adapted)

It is all too easy to allow interpretation of the event to be guided by Herodotos' near-incredulity at the Athenians being deceived by Peisistratos' 'ridiculous trick'. They were, as he points out, a people characterised among the Greeks for their rationality. But if we unpack the various religious and mythical messages presented in the act, we may arrive at a sense of why Peisistratos was able to behave as he did and why the people's response was so favourable. It should be noted at the outset that Herodotos' characterisation is only a partial one. However rational the Athenians were regarded as being, they were also distinguished among the Greeks for their devotion to their gods (Deacy 2007: esp. 234–5). This event of the 550s is indicative of the religiosity that was integral to their reputation.

For one thing, the act appealed to the Athenians' conviction that they had a special connection with Athena. The belief that Athena was willing to act on the city's behalf had been expressed in Solon's poem of some decades earlier. Peisistratos seems to be drawing on this belief by staging an epiphany of the goddess at another time of crisis. We also need to take account of the impact that the Great Panathenaia would have had upon the Athenians as a worshipping group. By the time of this event, the festival would have been celebrated three times: in 566, 562 and 558. Peisistratos would have been able to appeal to the renewed sense of communality provided by the festival, with much of its excitement generated by the impromptu ceremony.

The chariot ride of Peisistratos and 'Athena' also works at the interplay of ritual and myth. Peisistratos was effectively asserting himself as a successor of the heroes of old, who, championed by Athena, were able to succeed in their various endeavours. The choice of a chariot as a means of conveying Peisistratos and Phye even suggests one particular heroic parallel, Herakles, who as we have seen (Chapter 4) was depicted riding in a chariot alongside Athena in representations of his apotheosis. Peisistratos was possibly even presenting himself as a second Erichthonios given that one of that hero's innovations was the invention of chariot-riding (e.g. Fulgentius, *Mythologiae* 2.14).

Did the people believe that Phye was Athena? Possibly Herodotos is right and the people were taken in. If so, this shows Athenians to have been exceedingly receptive to religious feeling. Alternatively, they may have been willing victims of Peisistratos' ruse, choosing to participate in a communal event evoking the mythic companionship between the goddess and her favoured individuals. On this interpretation, the symbolic appeal of Athena becomes apparent, with the people celebrating her unifying potential by paying homage to the tyrant and the woman impersonating her.

Archaic Greek tyrants were typically responsible for building programmes. Under Peisistratos and his sons, Athens came to be beautified on unprecedented scale with the Akropolis summit emerging as a kind of showpiece. The most important building constructed on the Akropolis was the temple of Athena Polias (incidentally the only sixth-century building on the Akropolis whose foundations are still visible). It is possible that the temple was begun as late as around 525, under Peisistratos' sons, although an earlier date during Peisistratos' reign is more likely. The Peisistratid emphasis upon Athena confirmed the goddess' place as the foremost being in the religious system. Her role as an emblem of the city dates from the Peisistratid tyranny too. The Athena/owl coin type made its first appearance possibly around the time of Peisistratos' emergence to prominence in the 560s, although it may have been the innovation of his sons.

Under the Peisistratids, Athens became a cultural sensation with Athena as the symbol and embodiment of this newly developed confidence. Nothing would dampen this, not even the fall of the tyranny. Work on the temple of Zeus to the southeast of the Akropolis was halted after the overthrow of Hippias, presumably because, as a project, it was too closely linked with the tyrants. In contrast, the Peisistratid development of the Akropolis summit continued under the democracy. Athena had been presented as the special patron of Peisistratos, but also of the people as a whole. One of the legacies of the tyranny was a belief in an intimate bond between goddess and people that carried on through the end of the archaic period and into classical times.

THE PERSIAN INVASION

Athena's cult was so well established by the early fifth century BC that an event that ought perhaps to have shaken the Athenians' confidence in her patronage seems to have been turned into an opportunity to reassert her special concern for her people. In the aftermath of the victory over the Persians at Marathon in 490, work began on the 'Pre-Parthenon' or 'Older-Parthenon', a grand temple of Athena in commemoration of the victory. It was fated never to be finished, however, for when the Persians invaded Athens in 480, it was destroyed along with the other buildings of the Akropolis. What should have been impossible had taken place: the site that claimed Athena's special protection had been sacked, with the sanctuary that had been transformed in the previous century into one of the wonders of the Greek world left in ruins. This section will round off our discussion of Athena in early Athens by showing how, even with things at their most bleak, she was believed to use her powers on behalf of her people.

When the Persian invasion was imminent, an envoy was sent to Delphi to seek the advice of Apollo. The response, curiously unambiguous for an oracular pronouncement, calls the Athenians 'wretches', instructing them to 'fly from [their] houses and [their] city, flee to the end of the world'. So serious is their predicament, according to the oracle, that 'the head will not remain in its place, nor the body, nor the feet beneath . . . but all is ruined' (Herodotos 7.140.2–3). The Athenians refused to leave until they received a follow-up oracle. This, more favourable, pronouncement evokes Athena in her standard Athenian guises as patron of Athens and daughter of Zeus:

> Pallas is unable to appease great Olympian Zeus, though she beseeches him with many speeches and a shrewd metis . . . All will be taken and lost that the sacred border of Kekrops holds in keeping today . . . Yet a wooden wall built by all-seeing Zeus will be granted to Tritogeneia, a stronghold for you and your children. Do not await the host of horse and foot coming from Asia, nor be still, but turn your back and withdraw from the foe. Truly a day will come when you

will meet him face to face. Divine Salamis, you will bring death to women's sons
when the corn is scattered or the harvest gathered in.

(7.141.3–4)

At first, things still appear unpromising: Athena is envisaged as
interceding as best she can on the city's behalf but her attempts at
persuasion are having no effect; nor is her use of metis. All the
same, grounds for hope are offered by the grant to her of the
'wooden walls', a new 'stronghold' for the people. Heated discussion followed, Herodotos relates, as to how to interpret the oracle,
especially in light of the elusive reference to the 'wooden walls'.
Some thought that it denoted the Akropolis, which had once, it
was believed, been fenced by a thorn hedge (7.142), but the interpretation that found favour was the one proposed by Themistokles,
that it referred to the fleet. With the exception of a few dissenters
who stayed behind to defend the Akropolis, the people were
evacuated to the nearby island of Salamis. Athena's olivewood
statue seems to have left the city too, the only divine image known
to have been removed for safekeeping.

One day each year, Athena's olivewood image left the city to be
cleaned at the festival known as the Plynteria. In circumstances of
great secrecy, the peplos was removed as were the various orna-
ments that adorned it. It was then wrapped up and taken to the sea
at Phaleron to be washed. On this day on which the city temporarily
lost the image of its tutelary deity, Athens was an unhappy place.
Sanctuaries were shut and normal activities suspended. The
removal of Athena's image prior to the Persian invasion ought to
have been at least as portentous as the Plynteria, leaving as it did the
city unprotected in the face of an enemy invasion. But as it was,
an alternative stronghold was provided, the 'wooden walls' serving,
effectively, as a temporary Akropolis. Even when all looks lost, the
message seems to be, Athena was capable of finding a way of
interceding on her people's behalf. The cunning that enabled her
mythic protégés persistently to succeed against the odds is here
applied to the Athenians, the people who were thought, in the
ancient Greek world, to benefit from their bond with the goddess.

OVERVIEW

Athena's Akropolis cult was very old, possibly dating as far back as the Bronze Age. When Attica was unified under Athens, she came to be venerated as the major deity of city and territory alike. Thereafter, Athenian history and the history of Athena overlap. As Athens was emerging as a notable power in the sixth century, her cult was expanded with the institution of the Great Panathenaia and, subsequently, a major Akropolis building programme. She was evoked as the special patron of Peisistratos, whose tyranny elevated the city into a major player in the Greek world. Such was her connection with the city by the early fifth century that, even when her sanctuary was sacked, the Athenians found a way to characterise her as working on their behalf.

The sentiments expressed by Hegel, quoted at the head of this chapter, would be unthinkable for any other city. They constitute a rhetorical exaggeration but all the same capture a sense of how Athens' self image was connected with its patron deity.

ALL ABOUT ATHENA?
THE CLASSICAL AKROPOLIS

This . . . is more compact & splendid & robust than I remembered. The yellow pillars . . . gathered, grouped, radiating there on the rock . . . crowds flying as if suppliants . . . The temple, like a ship, so vibrant, taut, sailing, though still all these ages.

(Virginia Woolf, 21 April 1932, quoted in Woolf 1982: 90–1)

INTRODUCTION

During the fifth century, Athens emerged as the foremost political, economic and cultural power of the Greek world. In such a climate, its goddess flourished, with her major site of worship, the Akropolis summit, transformed into one of the wonders of the Greek world and her image joined with the political progress of the city. We will examine various of the statues and buildings constructed in her honour that testify to her power both as an image and as the tutelary deity of the city. Above all, we will consider the Parthenon, perhaps the greatest of all Greek temples. In tracing Athena's connections with Athens in the fifth century, we will be able to do something rarely possible in the study of any Greek god, namely to trace in some detail the role of cultural and historical factors in shaping their representations.

AFTER THE WARS

In the decades after the Persian Wars, the Akropolis buildings were left in ruins, with the cult image stored in a temporary shelter. All the same, a way was found to give thanks for the victories over the Persians. One of the triremes from the naval victory at Salamis was introduced into the procession at the Great Panathenaia. Placed on wheels, crewed by priests and priestesses, its most striking aspect was its sail, which appears to have been in the form of a massive peplos depicting the gigantomachy. This development to the festival gave a renewed significance to the mythic battle, which seems to have been reinterpreted in the aftermath of the Wars as a sort of forerunner to the Athenians' victory over their own 'barbarous' enemies.

In the years that followed, even though the buildings remained in ruins, the summit was adorned by the erection of powerful images of the goddess. The grandest of these was the nine-metre bronze statue by Pheidias built possibly between 460 BC and 450 BC that would have dominated the ruins until the rebuilding programme of the second half of the century. Financed by a tenth of the spoils of Marathon, it signalled a further attempt to commemorate that victory, succeeding where the ill-fated 'Pre-Parthenon' or 'Older Parthenon' of the immediate post-Marathon years (Chapter 6) had failed.

A very different image is another of Pheidias' statues, the bronze 'Lemnian Athena', dedicated around the middle of the century by a settlement of Athenian citizens sent to Lemnos. It was marked out in antiquity for a quality not normally associated with Athena: beauty. Lucian regarded 'the facial contour, its softness, and her well-proportioned nose' as among the features of the ideal woman (*Imagines* 6), while Himerios enthused in the fourth century AD about the 'rosy blush' of her cheeks (*Oratio* 68.4). Again the original bronze statue is lost, but it appears to have been bareheaded, probably gazing down at a helmet held in Athena's right hand. This appearance is what probably made it so appealing as an image of femininity, presenting a more peaceful, even demure or 'doe-eyed' Athena, with the downward gaze apparent also in representations

Figure 12 Athena Lemnia, Dresden, Staatliche Kunstsammlungen Hm 49, purchased from the Albani collection, Rome, in 1728.

of the birth of Erichthonios. The same sculptor who produced a martial image of Athena to dominate the summit also captured the other 'side' of Athena as the guardian of the Akropolis.

Athena has a similar downward gaze on another image from this period, the so-called 'Mourning Athena' from around 460 where, barefoot and aegis-less, she leans on her spear, looking down at an object before her. This object probably provides a key to interpreting the image, except that what it is remains unclear: a casualty list of the war dead perhaps, or a boundary stone setting out the limit of her sanctuary, or perhaps even the chest containing Erichthonios. Whichever is the case, it enables us to underscore the point that has been a recurrent feature of this chapter. In her role as Akropolis guardian, Athena was more than solely a warlike figure. In addition to her standard warlike image, she was envisaged as a caring and feminine, not to mention maternal, figure.

UNITY AND IMPERIALISM

By the middle of the fifth century, Athens had been transformed into a major Greek power with a large maritime empire known as the 'Delian League' after its original headquarters, the island of Delos. Athens had asserted its new-found power in 454 when the treasury of the league was transferred from Delos to the Akropolis. This development went in tandem with the elevation of the status of Athena, who now replaced Apollo, the major god of Delos, as the patron deity of the empire. This enhanced status impacted upon the Panathenaia in that each allied city was obliged to take part in the festival, providing a panoply and cow for the sacrifice and further enriching what must have been an already crowded sanctuary. The hekatomb on the altar of Athena would have been developed into an even greater spectacle, with the slaughter of the cattle lasting longer still, with extended ritual screaming. Athena's major festival was now elevated into an even greater celebration by incorporating the member cities of the empire into the communal celebration.

After the treasury of the Delian League was transferred to the Akropolis, the decision was made under the leadership of Perikles to embark on a rebuilding programme that turned the summit once again into one of the greatest cult sites of the Greek world. As under Peisistratos, Athena's symbolic and unifying potential was utilised, with messages about the goddess intertwined with messages about the city. The difference is that whereas we could only really speculate about the nature and extent of the Peisistratid building programme, this time we have significantly more evidence to trace the images of Athena that were presented, even though, at times, easy interpretation is impossible: indeed the sculptures have generated among the most varied, not to mention controversial, responses of any works from the ancient world.

The desire to present a unifying image of Athena is seen most strikingly in the 'Erechtheion', a major purpose of which was to replace the temple of Athena Polias destroyed by the Persians, hence its ancient name of 'the temple on the Akropolis in which the ancient image is'. Rather than in the exact location of the earlier temple (which, incidentally, is why the foundations of the earlier temple are still visible), it was built on the uneven terrain nearby that was the home of various cults including Poseidon-Erechtheus, Hephaistos, Pandrosos, Kekrops, Boutes (the ancestor of the Eteouboutid clan who provided the priesthoods of Athena Polias and Poseidon-Erechtheus), Zeus as both Hypatos ('most high') and Herkeios ('of the fence') and the guardian serpent. In place of a cluster of cults, an ingenious multi-level temple was constructed that at once honoured these cults by giving them a new home and hid them from view. In other words, it served a comparable function to the myths connected with the Akropolis that we surveyed in Chapter 5, drawing together various beings under the unifying image of Athena.

Another newly constructed building, the temple of Athena Nike, was doing something comparable. Situated in a little sanctuary on the edge of the Akropolis summit, just outside the entrance, the site had long-standing links with the goddess. With its own archaic cult statue, it honoured a separate cult from that of Athena Polias, although not, it would seem, originally a separate priesthood. Rather, the cult seems to have been administered by the priestess of Athena Polias until the 440s, when it acquired its own priesthood, drawn like all newly created priesthoods by lot rather than from an aristocratic family. As well as honouring Athena in her guise as the bringer of victory, the new temple made initial statements about the Akropolis for visitors about to enter the summit. Over the entrance to the temple, Athena was shown in the centre of a group of gods of the Akropolis including Aphrodite, Poseidon and Zeus. It introduced the revamped Akropolis by honouring other deities of the summit and slopes while emphasising the supremacy of Athena.

PRETTIFYING THE CITY: THE PARTHENON

Still greater visibility was given to Athena via the centrepiece of the project, the building known as the Parthenon (constructed 447–432). It is difficult not to describe this building in extravagant terms. The largest Doric temple ever built, its scale and quality are extraordinary. Not only is it among the greatest artistic achievements of Classical antiquity; it is also the only temple on which each of the (ninety-two) metopes were decorated with reliefs. It made an impression on visitors in antiquity, not least Herakleides of Krete who, in his third century BC *Notes on the Greek Cities*, recommended 'the magnificent temple of Athena, conspicuous and well worth a look, the so-called Parthenon'. The ruined site has enticed and astonished visitors since the late-eighteenth-century rediscovery of Greece, including Virginia Woolf, some of whose responses to seeing the Parthenon are quoted at the head of this chapter.

In attempting to recover ancient Athenian attitudes to the monument, however, we are frustrated by a lack of comments from the period of its construction. According to Plutarch, Perikles met with fervent criticism for using allied money to 'guild out the city, and to prettify her' (*Life of Perikles* 12), with the city even compared to a 'pretentious woman, decking herself out with expensive stones and statues and one-thousand talent temples'. In view of the emblematic significance of Athena by this time, it is tempting to infer that the goddess herself was being alluded to as a figure decked out like a woman in full make-up, with a beauty that, however striking, had been attained by artificial means.

Although it is among the best known temples from the ancient Greek world, it is not really a temple as we conventionally understand it. Remains were recently found of a small shrine within the building on the site of an older sanctuary, possibly of Athena Ergane. But it was never a major cult site. It seems not to have had a dedicated priestess, nor – more significantly – an altar. The major focus of Athena cult remained the north side of the rock, the home of the olivewood image and the great altar of Athena Polias. It also had a function that we might have difficulties regarding as religious in that one of its rooms housed the Athenian treasury. Rather than a religious building in the sense of a major cult site, it was more a kind of 'blank canvas' for the expression of messages about Athena and about the Athenian people as a worshipping group. These were controversial messages if the evidence from Plutarch is anything to go by, but also images on some level conducive to the democratic city in that, as with any other public building, its progress was subject to annual review by the assembly throughout the lengthy period of its construction.

It seems reasonable to assert, then, that the Athenians were saying something about their goddess and about her relationship with themselves. Indeed, it was unusual among temples of ancient Greece for the number of times it depicted a single deity, Athena, who appears on each of the pediments, on the metopes, and on the frieze running round the interior wall. Then, on entering the temple, visitors would be greeted with the ten-metre tall statue by Pheidias, a brilliant chryselephantine (gold and ivory) image of the goddess, in armour with helmet, shield and aegis, holding an image of Nike and with a serpent coiled inside the shield. Combined with this unusual focus upon a deity the building was unusual in depicting a non-heroic mortal scene on the frieze. The subject is a great procession on foot and horseback starting in the southwest corner and moving in two directions along the north and south, generally (though not exclusively: see below) seen as a depiction of the Athenian people celebrating Athena. Breaking from convention in this way and depicting people at worship, the temple was combining messages about Athena with messages about the Athenians as a worshipping group in a way that updated the connection between goddess and polis evident in the sixth century in ways that were conducive to the classical city at its peak.

A notable feature of the temple is its thematic consistency, with certain parts of the building in dialogue with others, repeating and developing particular religious and mythic ideas. We will now survey some of the themes, by looking at the pediments, the metopes beneath each of them, the frieze and finally the statue. As we will see, they present Athena as a patron of order and patriarchy while exploring her relationship with a range of images of femininity.

A convenient place to begin is the west side as, like today, this is the part of the building that visitors would be greeted with first, before moving round to the entrance at the east side. The west pediment displayed one of the principal foundation myths of Athens, the contest for the land (see Chapter 5). Below it, the metopes along the west side of the temple depicted Greeks (and possibly Athenians) fighting Amazons. Curious parallels and differences may be identified between the pediment and metopes in that each displays a male–female contest. Taken as a pair we are presented with females who enter Athens from the outside and seek control of the land, except that on the metopes, the women (Amazons) are going to lose, while on the pediment the female (Athena) will win. This juxtaposition of differing images of warrior femininity expresses a recurrent feature of Athena that we have been exploring in this book, that as the warrior female she ought to be subversive, but instead she devotes herself to 'the male' and to the well-being of the patriarchal city. This difference is reflected in the nature of the two arrivals. When Athena came to Athens, it was with the olive tree, a symbol of peace and prosperity, while the Amazons arrived intent on conquest. Athena's arrival benefits the city; the Amazons sought to replace patriarchy with female rule. We are presented almost with a visual depiction of the sentiments expressed by Athena in Aeschylus' *Eumenides*, produced in 459 BC, where, though she rejects marriage, she upholds the male 'in every respect ... with all my heart' (737, 8; see further Chapter 1).

The notion of Athena as supporter of order is consistent with her representation in the east pediment, which displayed her other mythic arrival, her birth. As we have seen, this was a powerful theme

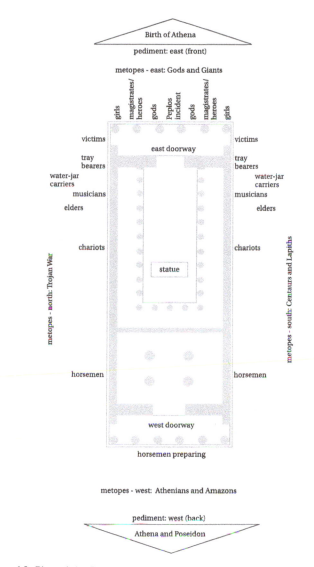

Figure 13 Plan of the Parthenon; drawing by Kate Morton; reproduced by kind permission of the artist.

Figure 14 East side of the Parthenon Frieze 29–37, London, British Museum.

for the Athenians. The event that established her intimacy with Zeus, it was one of the mythic events commemorated at the Panathenaia. Most of the sculpture has been long destroyed, although it appears that Zeus stood in the centre with the newly born Athena beside him and various gods arranged on either side. The pediment seems to be conveying the effects of the birth upon the cosmos via the depiction, at each corner, of Helios rising and Selene (the moon) descending.

As for the metopes beneath it, once again a mythic connection is apparent, the theme being the gigantomachy. This has the effect of underlining the connection between Athena and Zeus, while reinforcing the Panathenaia theme since, as we have seen, the gigantomachy was one of the myths commemorated at the festival.

In addition to depictions of myths connected with the Panathenaia, further allusions to the festival are presented on the frieze,
which probably presents an idealised representation of the Panathenaic procession and elements of the Panathenaic Games,
although other suggestions include that it represents the Marathon
dead. The procession converges on the east side above the entrance
where the twelve Olympian gods are shown in two groups of six,
culminating, to one side, with Hera and Zeus and, to the other, with
Athena and Hephaistos (figure 14). This provides a means of linking
the king and queen of Olympos with the major divine couple of
Athenian religion, the parents of Erichthonios. At the same time, it
reinforces the link between Athena and Zeus presented on the east
pediment by depicting each deity at the head of a group of gods.

Between Zeus and Athena, in the part of the frieze that would have stood over the entrance to the temple, some kind of religious ritual is taking place involving two girls with cushioned stools on their heads who are approaching a woman (the priestess of Athena Polias?) who seems to be about to take the stool from the girl nearer her. Next to them a child, generally – though not always – identified as a boy, is being handed a large piece of folded cloth by a man (perhaps the archon basileus, the head of Athenian state religion). The object is seen as providing a key to interpreting the scene if not the whole frieze. It is usually taken to be the new peplos presented to Athena at the Panathenaia, an interpretation especially appealing as Athena has removed her aegis, in readiness perhaps to receive the new robe. The problem that has been raised with this possibility is that the gods are looking away, leading some to question a Panathenaic interpretation. In the early 1990s, the interpretation of the frieze was much discussed among academics and in the media following a theory proposed by Joan Breton Connelly (published in Connelly 1996) that the frieze depicts one of Athens' local myths, the story of Erechtheus and his daughters.

Erechtheus, as we saw in the previous chapter, emerges from the Homeric poems as, effectively, a doublet of Erichthonios, born as he was out of the earth, reared by Athena and taken into her temple. Elsewhere, he is, instead, the descendent of Erichthonios, a separate mythic being with his own experiences, albeit ones that echo those of his ancestor. A son of Poseidon called Eumolpos had, according to the story, declared war on Athens because he wanted to establish his father as its patron deity. Athens, at that time, was ruled by Erechtheus who, together with his family, saved the city thanks to their devotion, which saw them put its well-being before any personal feelings or family affiliations. The fragmentary *Erechtheus* of Euripides, possibly to be dated to the late 420s, related how Erechtheus was told by oracle that in order to save the city he needed to sacrifice one of his daughters. The girl, whose name is not known from the surviving fragments of the play, nor from any other source, duly offered her life, supported by her mother Praxithea. In a display of extreme sisterly unity, the girls, also unnamed, killed themselves apparently having made a pledge to die as a group. In the ensuing battle, Eumolpos was killed. Erechtheus fell victim to Poseidon, who subsequently produced an earthquake that made the ground swallow him up. The surviving family member, Praxithea, was rewarded for her devotion to the city by being made the first priestess of Athena Polias.

Through a detailed reading of the Parthenon frieze, Connelly posited a link between each of the figures and objects in the scene and various characters in the myth. The man is identified by her as Erechtheus getting reading to sacrifice his daughter; the cloth is the funeral shroud; the child next to him is his youngest daughter; the other children are the other daughters; the woman, according to Connelly, is their mother, Praxithea, who was eventually instated by Athena as the first priestess of Athena Polias.

Interpreted in this manner, the frieze presents images appropriate to a temple that honours both Athena and Athens through a depiction of patriotic Athenians, all willing to put Athens first, ranging from Erechtheus who died defending the city, the self-sacrificing daughters, and Praxithea, the mother who was willing to put the city before her family. Connelly's theory also offers an explanation for why it is that the gods are turning their back on the mortals rather than watching what is going on: such an event, it is argued, would be repugnant to them. There have been cogent criticisms of the theory, however. The child being handed the cloth is generally considered to be a boy rather than a girl. But what probably renders the theory untenable is the absence of two vital ingredients for a sacrificial scene, a knife and an altar.

Connelly's theory demonstrates how open the Parthenon frieze is to a range of readings. I should like now to consider one further possibility, namely that the rite being depicted is the Arrhephoria, the festival when, according to Pausanias, two girls, directed by Athena's priestess, made a nocturnal journey each year in what may have been a re-enactment of the events surrounding the birth of Erichthonios (see Chapter 5). A connection with the Arrhephoria may be further discerned if we look at the arrangement of Athena and Hephaistos to the right of the religious ritual. Athena is interested in her fellow god rather than in the mortals, making eye-contact with him while holding the aegis over her lap. Her gesture is a defensive one, perhaps alluding to their sexual encounter, the mythic event that links them as Athenian gods and the event that led to the conception of Erichthonios.

If the origins of Erichthonios are being alluded to, a Panathenaic interpretation is not thereby excluded: the story about Erichthonios was after all the story of the mythic founder of the festival. The sculpture appears to be evoking a number of mythic and religious statements about the gods and heroes of the Athenians notably Athena, Hephaistos and Erichthonios. It also seems to be depicting the Athenians' own participation in the worship of these beings at the Panathenaia and possibly at the Arrhephoria.

Finally, we will examine what the statue of Athena Parthenos adds to our interpretation. A striking image of Athena in its own right, it takes on more significance still when we think about its relationship with the sculpture of the temple. Its shield was richly decorated, on the inside with gods fighting giants, on the outside depicting the Amazonomachy, echoing the metopes along the eastern and western sides of the building, which as we have seen exemplify Athena's associations with the promotion of civilised (divine/Greek/Athenian) order and peace. Once again, she is connected with the defeat of these women, her 'good' warrior femininity being contrasted to the dangerous and troubling femininity of the Amazons. As for the serpent, it could be either the guardian serpent of the Akropolis, or a representation of Erichthonios in his serpentine guise. This would help explain why the shield appears to be offering protection to the serpent, who is coiled up inside it. Athena's martial and nurturing femininity are usually kept separate. Here they are blended together. The goddess resplendent in her armour is also the protector of the guardian serpent who might also be her son.

The base of the statue depicted the birth of Pandora, the first woman/wife, who unleashed all evils into the world when she opened the chest with which she had been entrusted. A powerful image for the Greeks, Pandora exemplified 'woman', being at once beautiful and exotic on the one hand but evil on the other. She is, in Hesiod's *Theogony* the *kalon kakon* (585) or 'beautiful evil', at

Figure 15 Athena Parthenos model (plaster), c. 1970 AD, Royal Ontario Museum 962.228.16. With permission of the Royal Ontario Museum © ROM.

once enticing and disastrous. Her birth may seem an unusual choice of mythic theme for the statue's base, but it is appropriate in several respects. Athena played a part in her creation as we have seen, when after Hephaistos had created her out of clay and water, she taught her woolworking (see p. 52). Then there is her container, the storage jar that has long been misidentified as her 'box'. The chest that is opened in disobedience is a theme of the Erichthonios story, which may explain the mistake by one of the sources (Fulgentius *Mythologiae* 2.14), which identifies three daughters of Kekrops as Herse, Aglauros and Pandora.

In a seminal article 'What is a goddess?', Nicole Loraux (1992) proposed two possibilities, that a goddess is either to be understood as simply the feminine version of a god, or that her femininity is key to how she is to be interpreted. If the second possibility is true, then it is necessary to consider whether her femininity is the same as mortal women's or whether it is more intense or more extreme in some way. These questions offer a route to understanding the intriguingly gendered persona of Athena. Variously presented as warrior, eternal virgin, mother and protectress, she blends together a range of feminine traits in ways that would be impossible in the mortal world. These varied images of femininity are presented in the sculpture of the Parthenon which imbues Athena with traits of the most notorious women of myth, the Amazons and Pandora, who exemplify woman as appealing and dangerous. As a goddess, however, she transcends them as patron god of the polis.

OVERVIEW

In the fifth century, Athens expressed its new-found pre-eminence by transforming the Akropolis into a celebration of goddess and polis. The city drew on the unifying potential of Athena already evident in the archaic period, celebrating not only the goddess but also the people themselves. The 'goddess of nearness' who intervenes in the lives of favoured individuals of myth is evoked here in association with the Athenian people as a worshipping group. While being all about Athena, the Akropolis presents an idealised view of the Athenian people too. This chapter has shed further light upon the complexity of Athena from a gendered perspective. The Parthenon in particular has been seen to present varied images of the goddess, ranging from the masculine warrior to the nurturer, while contrasting her brand of femininity with the mortal models she evokes but also transcends.

8

THE WIDER GREEK WORLD

Hail, goddess, and look after Inachian Argos. Hail both when you drive out, and
when you drive back again your horses, and preserve all the estate of the
Danaans.

(Kallimachos, *The Bath of Pallas* 140–2, tr. Morrison)

INTRODUCTION

Although Athena was intimately associated with Athens as its patron
and symbol, she was also worshipped in the wider Greek world,
throughout the cities of the mainland and islands and also in the
peripheries of Greek influence to the east and west. This chapter
will be concerned with perceptions and cults of Athena in various
cities and regions. We will attempt to recover distinctive aspects of
the goddess in some of her places of worship while considering how
far aspects that we have explored in Chapters 1–7 are evident in
particular localities.

We have been in a privileged position in examining Athena's
Athenian manifestations. There is sufficient evidence to examine
her place in the religious system and to trace how her worship
developed over time. Looking beyond Athens in contrast entails
dealing with scattered references and pieces of archaeological data
that do not lend themselves to easy analysis. Frequently we are
faced with little more than frustrating and tantalising glimpses

of local cults and traditions. In some instances, there is only a collection of epithets (or even just one or two) to go on, which are risky to use as a starting point for the reconstruction of a cult, let alone for a sense of how cults developed across time. Sometimes a story is linked with a sanctuary, but this often complicates the picture rather than offering solutions, especially as the source is very often Pausanias. A major source for local cults, he describes sanctuary layouts, lists epithets and recounts stories connected with sites, but we need to be wary of regarding him as an accurate record. Not only is he a late author, who flourished around AD 150; he also presents Greek myths as curiosities, with the result that how far they pertain to cultic realities is a moot point. There is the question, too, of how he obtained his information, whether, for example, he may at times have been misled by tour guides who gave inaccurate information concerning particular local features and customs. He will be adduced regularly below, because without him, our knowledge would be even patchier, but each time he needs to be used with caution.

Rather than attempting to list every extant representation of the goddess and every site at which she is known to have been worshipped, we will focus upon a selection of sites in mainland Greece and in the islands. We will also examine her cults on the peripheries of the Greek world, taking account of how interactions with non-Greek peoples impacted upon representations of her, including Egyptians, Phoenicians and Romans, whose deity Minerva became so successfully assimilated with Athena that the goddesses became in certain respects interchangeable.

MOVING BEYOND ATHENS

In spite of Athens' political and cultural dominance, its influence on the cult practices of other states was minimal. Even when Athens was flourishing as an imperial power, it seems not to have impacted upon the religious practices of the subject cities. What we do see is the use of Athena as symbol of Athenian power. In various locations, including Aegina and Samos, there is evidence for the establishment of precincts of *Athena Athenōn Medeousa* ('Athena queen of Athens'), probably marking land that had been confiscated from revolting cities. Far from interfering in the religious life of the cities, Athena is being used in order to denote Athenian power in these places.

Athena's emblematic status in Athens did not prevent her from being an important deity elsewhere, even locations with a hostile relationship with Athens. She was the national goddess of Boiotia, for example, the region whose relationship with neighbouring Attica was frequently troubled, with major sanctuaries at Koroneia (the Itoneion) and Alalkomenai. The crow, presented as Athena's enemy in Athenian myth (see Chapter 5), may have been Athena's attribute in Boiotia, possibly paralleling the status of the owl in Athens (Deacy 1995: 98). Athens' enmity with Sparta in the fifth century, meanwhile, appears not to have weakened Athena's place in Spartan religion; in fact, as we will see, there is evidence for distinctive cult activity in her sanctuary on the akropolis of Sparta in the classical period.

Another point we need to be clear on is that Athens was far from typical in its mode of worship of Athena. There are distinct similarities, the most obvious of which we will consider first, and others of which we will trace throughout the chapter. But there are also certain fundamental differences, which this chapter will outline and explain.

Athena's major cult title at Athens was found widely throughout Greece. Numerous cities possessed cults of Athena Polias, including Argos, Troizen and Stymphalos, while similar epithets including Poliatis, Poliouchos and Polemadoke ('war-sustaining') are attested at Tegea, Sparta and Koroneia respectively. Other epithets appear to have functioned as equivalents of Polias, including Alalkomeneia ('she who wards off' or 'protectress') at Mantineia and at Alalkomenai in Boiotia, and Hyperdexia ('protectress of the people'), attested mainly in the islands. As at Athens, Athena sanctuaries were frequently situated on akropoleis: those of Sparta, Gythion, Leuktra, Argos, Mycenae, Troizen, Tegea, Lindos, Haliartos, Koukounaries on Paros, and Cumae to name but a few. It might almost be said that wherever there was an akropolis, there was a cult of Athena. Even in places where an akropolis was lacking, the highest available point could be selected for an Athena sanctuary as may be seen in the case of Megalopolis in Arcadia. When it was founded in the fourth century BC, Athena was given a sanctuary on a hill, the closest thing to an akropolis in the new city.

As we have seen, Athena was at once the principal deity of the Athenian pantheon and also Athens' figurehead, with her helmeted head depicted on its coins, together with the owl and the olive branch, the latter of which evoked her protection as well as her victory over Poseidon in the contest for the land. This figurative status was not restricted to Athens. Other cities' coins depict an armed Athena, including Troizen, Argos, and in the best-known instance, Corinth. On the Corinthian staters, Athena is shown on the obverse wearing a Corinthian helmet, while Pegasos, the winged horse, appears on the reverse. Pegasos may have held value as a symbol because of his connections with Athena, who, as we have seen, helped bring about his birth from the head of the Gorgon. There was, in addition, a local dimension to the connection in that Bellerophon, who, with Athena's help, tamed Pegasos (p. 48), was a local Corinthian hero.

Aspects of Athena present in Athenian cult, then, are discernible elsewhere in the Greek world. We should not, however, let Athena's status as protectress and figurehead obscure some fundamental differences between the sacred geography of Athens and of other cities. As we have seen, Athens was a centrally administered, 'monocentric' city whose major urban sanctuary was the chief cult of the whole polis whereas most cities were 'bipolar', with their major sanctuaries situated in peripheral locations often some distance from the urban centre. The purpose of these sanctuaries was to serve as gathering places for the community, and to assert the community's control over the agricultural land. The chief sanctuary of Sparta, for example, that of Apollo Hyakinthos, was at Amyklai around five kilometres away, while Argos' major cult site, the Heraion, was eight kilometres away in the Argolid. Like many great sanctuaries, the Heraion was in a strategic location, in the vicinity of the territories of two other poleis. It was located nine

Figure 16 Map of Greece, showing key sites discussed in Chapter 8.

kilometres from Tiryns and a mere five kilometres from Mycenae. Athena was a prominent deity of both Argos and Sparta, with important urban sanctuaries, but in neither location was she the principal deity of the pantheon. Studying Athena outside Athens involves setting aside the notion of the goddess as patron of the 'monocentric' city that guided our discussion throughout Chapters 5–7.

SPARTA: THE BRONZE HOUSE AND THE BELLS

We will begin with Sparta as an instance of an Athena cult that appears to have had importance for the local worshipping group, but for which our knowledge is frustratingly limited. At Athena's temple on the akropolis of Sparta, the goddess was known by two epithets, one of which – Poliouchos – is attested elsewhere, and denotes her role as protectress of the city. The other, Chalkioikos, appears to be local to Sparta. It means 'of the bronze house' but why her temple should be the 'bronze house' is far from clear. One possibility is that the cult statue is indicated, which, according to Pausanias, was made of bronze (3.17.2). Another is that the walls of the temple were decorated with bronze plaques, a possibility supported by the archaeological findings from the site, which include a number of bronze plates and nails. Thirdly, the epithet may point to one of Athena's roles in Sparta, her patronage of bronze metalworkers.

An intriguing feature of worship at the temple is attested, namely the use of bells, of which a large number have been excavated, around 120 in total, mostly in terracotta and others in bronze, predominantly from the classical period. As far as is known, this type of object is unique in the worship of Athena: at no other site are bells known to have been dedicated to her. We can arrive at a guess as to their purpose from examining uses of bells in other contexts in the ancient Greek world, including to guard cities and to ward off enemies in battle. The most plausible explanation is an apotropaic one, with the noise of ringing bronze serving to ward off evil. If so, Athena Chalkioikos may have functioned as a specialised version of Athena Poliouchos, with her protective role linked with the clanging sound of the bells. This is an inviting suggestion given that Athena is associated with the creation of noise elsewhere, the war cry on occasion of her birth, for example, or a song for the aulos song that she was considered to have composed from the death lament of the Gorgon (e.g. Pindar, *Pythian Odes* 12.18–27). This leads us to another possible explanation for the name of the temple, that it derived from the noise of bells emanating from it.

From the little evidence we have to go on for Sparta, we have gleaned tantalising glimpses of Athena's cult. The goddess is apparent in her standard guise of protectress, although with distinctive local aspects to this role. We will turn now to Argos, bringing in Tegea for brief comparison. We are more fortunate in one respect than we were with Sparta in that we hear of local traditions that may aid in our interpretation of the cult, although the evidence must be used with care deriving as it does from authors whose work needs to be used cautiously.

ARGOS: 'CLEAR-SIGHTED ATHENA'

While Hera presided over the Argolid from her great sanctuary, the Heraion, Athena was the protectress of the urban space, worshipped on the main akropolis, Larisa, as Polias and on the other hill, Aspis, as Oxyderkes ('with penetrating gaze' or 'clear-sighted'), an epithet attested only at Argos.

The foundation of the sanctuary of Athena Oxyderkes was credited to Diomedes, Pausanias (2.24.2) tells us, in gratitude to Athena for 'lifting the mist from his eyes' to inspire his warrior prowess on the battlefield at Troy. This looks like a rather forced attempt to link Diomedes' exploits with the cult of his city, although this is not the only instance of his Trojan deeds figuring in Argive myth and cult. Argos was the home of the palladion statue, believed to have been taken to Argos by Diomedes after he stole it from Troy, thereby transferring Athena's magical protection from Troy to his own city. This story parallels other traditions connected with Athena that drew attention to her ability to confer inviolability. In Arcadia, the city of Tegea claimed to possess a lock of the Gorgon's hair, originally belonging to Athena, but which became the property of a local princess, Sterope (Apollodoros 2.7.3). The lock was to be kept in a bronze jar unless the city were to be attacked, when Sterope should hold it up three times from the city walls, and the enemy would be put to flight. This story points us again to the maxim we have explored already in this book, that to have Athena on your side is to achieve success. It is for this reason that, far from having negative associations, Diomedes' theft was depicted on Argive coins, with the palladion on the reverse, at once celebrating the local hero's actions and advertising the city's special protection.

The theme of sight figures intriguingly in a cult of Athena at Argos described in the *Bath of Pallas* by the Hellenistic poet Kallimachos (*Hymn* 5, especially 51–4; 82–9) which recounts a procession of young women to bathe the statue of Pallas (= the palladion?) in the river Inachos. One of the most striking aspects of the rite is the requirement that men should keep away lest they should see the goddess naked and be blinded. This requirement is clarified by means of the story of Teiresias, the young man who happened upon Athena naked and had his sight taken away by the goddess. He had seen something that no man should, namely the naked body of the virgin goddess. This is the goddess who, after all, was thought not even to have been naked when born, but to have emerged adorned in her armour. The bathing of Pallas recalls the Athenian rite, the Plynteria, when Athena's statue was taken to the sea to be bathed. Not only was there secrecy surrounding the Athenian festival, but it was a day of ill omen (Chapter 6), involving as it did the removal of the attributes of the goddess who, of all the deities, is defined by what she wears: her armour and dress.

It is necessary that we resist the temptation to assume that Kallimachos' poem reflects cultic reality. A Hellenistic poem rich in literary devices, it could be read as further evidence of associations between sight and the Argive cult of Athena, or as an elaboration upon aspects of Argive cult by a learned author. It demonstrates the potential dangers connected with local cults in that tempting though it is to seize upon each piece of evidence as information about local perceptions or worship, we need to remain aware of the limitations of many of our sources.

As in the case of Sparta, we have been far from conclusive: we have only been able to propose some suggestions that seem to do the best justice to such evidence that we possess. From piecing together such evidence that exists, it appears that at Argos there were particular dimensions to Athena's role as protectress deriving from the magical palladion, and connected with the power of her gaze.

ARCADIA: A FERTILITY GODDESS?

The sanctuary of Athena Alea ('shelter', 'asylum'), at Tegea in south-east Arcadia, housed one of the most celebrated cults of Athena. Among the most famous of ancient Greek sanctuaries, it played host to, among others, the Sparta kings Leotychidas and Pausanias. It housed a thriving cult site in the eighth century BC, although evidence of earlier worship is also apparent. A large temple, constructed in the seventh century, was burnt down in the fourth century. Its successor, 'a temple both large and worth seeing' (Pausanias 8.45.4), was regarded as the most impressive in the Peloponnese. We possess more evidence for the sanctuary than for many other sites of Athena worship because it has been extensively excavated, most recently by the Norwegian team that has been excavating the site since the 1990s.

The sanctuary's main source of interest for our survey of Athena cults is that it runs counter to the standard pattern of Athena worship. The cult was in a peripheral location, situated not on an akropolis but in the plain away from the urban centre. It fits the pattern of most great sanctuaries in being situated at a strategic location, here the crossroads between Arcadia and the Argolid. But what was a major sanctuary of Athena doing in a suburban setting? Can we discern anything distinctive about the local identity of Athena in Tegea? Does this add to our understanding of Athena as she was perceived and worshipped in the Greek world?

A story connected with the sanctuary points to distinctive conceptions of the goddess at Tegea. It concerns a local woman, Auge, the priestess of Athena Alea, who was raped by Herakles and gave birth to Telephos in the sanctuary, beside its sacred fountain (e.g. Apollodoros 2.7.4; Pausanias 8.457). Athena's anger is hardly surprising. The only birth that should take place in a site associated with her is her own, beside a local river Triton. Also, Athena's anger is attested against other women who defile her sanctuaries, namely Medusa and another priestess, Iodama, who entered her major Boiotian sanctuary, the Itoneion at night (Pausanias 9.34.2) and was startled by the aegis. In some respects, then, the story fits the wider picture of Athena myths and cults. It is Athena's response to the sacrilege that makes the story distinctive in that it gives her what might be termed 'fertility' characteristics. She was said to have brought about a plague and made the earth sterile, actions normally connected with 'fertility' deities, the most celebrated example being Demeter when she withdrew her power to make the crops grow in the aftermath of the abduction of Persephone.

From this story, Athena Alea emerges as a deity envisaged differently from the standard image of the goddess, with characteristics more normally associated with Demeter. The archaeological evidence seems to confirm a distinctive conceptualisation of Athena. Included among the votive offerings that have been unearthed at the sanctuary are swords, shields and arrowheads, which accord with the standard, warrior image of the goddess. Among the earlier objects that have been found are ones normally linked with deities commonly classified as 'fertility' gods, notably Demeter and Persephone. These include pomegranate pendants, numerous of which have been found at the sanctuary (Voyatzis 1998: 139; 140). Like all objects used in religious contexts in ancient Greece, the Spartan bells for instance, the precise significance of the pomegranate is difficult to pin down. Given its connections with Demeter and Persephone, however, a connection with fertility and life after death seems to be most likely.

This raises the possibility that, early on, Athena Alea had traits more commonly associated with Demeter than with Athena. This testifies, perhaps, to a time when the perception of Athena had not taken its later, panhellenic character. The apparent early image of the goddess might help shed light on the location of the sanctuary. Athena Alea was, perhaps, the protectress of the agricultural land rather than the urban centre. The story about Auge might suggest that Athena Alea continued to be envisaged as a 'fertility' power at least in local myth.

Our examination of the sanctuary of Athena Alea has shown that we should avoid over-simple statements about the nature of Athena and her worship. While usually associated with urban areas, one of her most famous sanctuaries – the greatest perhaps after the Athenian Akropolis – was situated in the plain and seems to point to a conceptualisation of the goddess that differs from that which we normally connect with her. We will consider another non-urban sanctuary of Athena in the next section, that at Delphi.

DELPHI AND ELSEWHERE: THE CONCEPTION AND PROTECTION OF CHILDREN

One of the most distinctive aspects of Athena in Athens is her association with Erichthonios, whose extraordinary conception and birth is due largely to her, and whom she strives to protect by placing him in a chest and eventually rearing him in her temple. This section will end our survey of Athena cults in cities and regions of Aegean Greece by exploring Athena's links with childbirth at other sites, beginning with her role in the birth of Apollo. In some versions of the myth of Apollo's birth, Athena is said to have loosened the girdle of Leto to enable her to give birth. One account (Pausanias 1.31.1) locates this act at a place called Zoster ('Girdle') on the coast of Attica. Leto then went on to Delos, the site of the birth of Apollo and Artemis.

At Delphi, too, Athena may have been envisaged in this role. The major god of Delphi was Apollo, whose sanctuary on the slopes of Mount Kithaeron was one of the major panhellenic cult sites. Athena's sanctuary was some distance away on lower ground at Marmaria, the site of a temple distinguished for its size and beauty (Demosthenes, 25 [*Against Aristogeiton* 1].34). The tholos (figure 17), popular on postcards from Delphi (sometimes erroneously identified as the 'temple of Apollo'), was one of the buildings in the sanctuary, although its purpose is unknown. As Athena Pronaia ('before the temple'), she functioned as guardian of the temple of Apollo. That she seems to have had the role of guardian of the god himself may be indicated by the presence in the sanctuary of an altar of Athena Zosteria ('of the girdle') which may recall the assistance that Athena gave Apollo's mother Leto in childbirth.

On the face of it, it may look curious that the virgin Athena should have been linked with childbirth. The notion of a virgin goddess with power over childbirth, however, is attested widely in Greece and beyond, in the Greek Artemis, for example, or the

Figure 17 The sanctuary of Athena at Marmaria, with the temple of Apollo on higher ground above; photo: Daniel Dench.

Roman Diana, the logic being that the deities' untapped sexuality invested them with sexual power. As a goddess who withholds her sexuality, Athena is ideally suited to solve problems with conception or childbirth. What lies behind Athena's interventions that enable the production of children is not so much a safeguarding of childbirth *per se*, but an ability to allow individuals to be born in unusual circumstances, from her own 'son' Erichthonios to Apollo and Artemis, whose birth had been prevented by Hera until Athena's intervention that enabled the children to be born. With this in mind, let us turn briefly to a story told by Pausanias (5.3.2) about a sanctuary of Athena in Elis:

> The women of Elis, it is said, prayed to Athena to make them conceive as soon as they next slept with their husbands because the country was deprived of its youth. Their prayer was answered, and they established a sanctuary of Athena

Meter ('mother') and because both wives and husbands experienced extreme
delight in their union, they called the place Bady ('sweet').

Again, it is due to Athena that children come to be born when
circumstances had been preventing this. The Orphic literature, too,
draws on these abilities of Athena, here in relation to Dionysos. The
young god had been lured away from his protectors, the Kouretes,
by the Titans, who killed him, dismembered his body and ate him
(West 1983: 74.) But Athena managed to get hold of his still-beating
heart, which she placed in a chest, out of which the god was reborn.
Dionysos, the 'Twice-born' god here has a third birth under Athena's
patronage out of his still-beating heart.

Athena was herself born in strange circumstances: contained in
the body of Zeus until the blow from Hephaistos' axe allowed her
to leap forth. She is involved, too, in the production of children in
comparably strange circumstances. Pegasos and Chrysaor emerge
from the severed neck of Medusa in a way that comes closest in
myth to her own emergence. Chrysaor especially evokes Athena
in the manner of his birth in that he is born as a warrior. His name,
'Golden Sword', is also fitting for a figure who emerges in armour,
paralleling perhaps the dazzling display of Athena's birth.

When Athena functions as a goddess involved in childbirth, what
she brings to bear is her capacity as a situation inverter. This provides us with yet another instance of her role as the power able to
bring about what was seemingly impossible, here the production
of children in unusual circumstances.

ASSIMILATIONS: ANAT AND MINERVA

Reconstructing cults of Athena in the Greek world has presented
particular challenges including piecing together from scanty evidence the meanings that she would have had for her worshippers
at the various sites. We face a new set of problems when we move
to the more peripheral areas of Greek influence, namely gauging
the extent to which Athena came to be assimilated with certain
goddesses of other ancient peoples.

Ancient polytheistic cultures were readily willing to make links between their gods and those of other peoples. Deities did not need to be identical in every respect, just to have enough elements in common to lead to an identification being made. Neith, the warrior/weaver goddess of Sais in Egypt, for example, was connected to Athena by various ancient authors even though some of her traits – her crocodile-appearance for one thing – lacked a parallel with Athena. Plato's *Timaeus* for one, asserts that the founder of Sais is said to be 'a goddess whose Egyptian name is Neith and in Greek, as they assert, Athena' (21e), while Herodotos (e.g. 2.28, 59, 182) consistently refers to the goddess of Sais by the name of Athena.

Neith and Athena were goddesses of separate religious systems with enough similar traits to enable them to be equated. Where another deity, Anat, was concerned, the connection went a stage further because of the long tradition of interactions between Greeks and Phoenicians on the island of Cyprus. Cyprus was distinguished in the ancient world for being a 'melting pot' of civilisations, inhabited early on by the indigenous inhabitants alongside Phoenicians, Greeks and others. It was a religious melting pot, too, with a pantheon comprising gods of the various peoples. In such a climate, assimilations were common, between Herakles and the Phoenician god Melqart, for instance, and between Apollo and the Phoenician Resheph.

As for Athena, by the fifth century at the latest and possibly considerably earlier, she was connected with Anat, the 'virgin' and 'destroyer' of the Phoenicians, a goddess distinguished for her ferocity and among whose attributes was the axe. Anat was also, like Athena, the daughter of a powerful father, in her case El, and her remits as a goddess included the protection of cities. As ever, the 'fit' between the goddesses was not a perfect one in that Anat possessed some distinctively un-Athena like traits in that she was characteristically represented as horned and winged. However, the perceived connection between the goddesses was such that they were worshipped jointly at Idalion and at a site now known as Larnaka-tis-Lapethou. The extent of their assimilation may be discerned by a bilingual Greek and Phoenician inscription on a fourth-century BC inscription on an altar found at Larnaka-tis-Lapethou which was dedicated in Greek to 'Athena Soteria (Salvation) Nike and King Ptolemy for good fortune' and in Phoenician to 'Anat, force of life, and the King of Kings Ptolemy for good fortune'.

This connection between Athena and her Phoenician counterpart seems to have been confined largely to Cyprus. An assimilation with a greater impact was that between Athena and the Roman goddess Minerva who was associated early on with Athena as part of the hellenising tradition in early Rome which identified Roman deities with their closest equivalents in the Greek pantheon. Like Athena, Minerva had a tutelary function, in her case as a member of the Capitoline Triad of Jupiter–Juno–Minerva. She was, in common with Athena, also a craft goddess, whose main Roman festival was the Quinquatrus, the festival of craftsmen. Another of her guises, Minerva Medica, evokes Athena Hygieia, in that she functioned as a healing goddess throughout Italy and in the wider Roman world, including Aquae Sulis (Bath), the home of the Romano-Celtic goddess Sulis Minerva.

The image of Athena had a major impact upon the iconography of Minerva, so much so that what Minerva looked like prior to her assimilation with Athena is not known. In terms of appearance then, the goddesses are identical. There is a linguistic affiliation too which parallels the Athena–Anat instance that we considered above, this time a bilingual inscription on a statue dedicated by a Roman merchant at Lindos in the third century BC to '*Athana [i Lindiai]*' and 'Minerva [i Lindiai]'. For 'Minerva', then in this regard read 'Athena'.

These long-standing associations should not blind us, however, to real differences in perceptions and worship between the two goddesses. Minerva never had the figurative importance of Athena and she was secondary in importance to her fellow deities in the Capitoline Triad. One of her major functions that is without a parallel in the Greek world concerned the overseeing of the transition to adulthood of children, especially girls, a role in the Greek world generally the domain of Artemis for girls, and Apollo for boys. Iconographically and mythologically, Athena and Minerva became identical, but they remained distinctive goddesses within their respective pantheons.

OVERVIEW: A MULTIPLICITY OF ATHENAS?

As at Athens, Athena functioned as city goddess throughout the Greek world, although our survey has demonstrated major departures from the Athenian model. Her status as city protectress did not make her the principal deity in the local pantheon, for the chief sanctuary was often situated away from the urban area. What is more, in those instances we have looked at, where her sanctuaries are the major ones of the city or region these are situated not on the akropolis, but before the settlement in an extra-urban location. This chapter has shown various ways in which Athena was worshipped throughout the Greek world, while providing further confirmation of the unusual nature of her cult at Athens.

The worship of Athena was marked by its diversity as befits a world comprising numerous independent city states each with their own pantheons, local heroes and sacred geography. Each city or region worshipped her in a manner that suited its particular local circumstances, a tendency that holds for the Aegean Greek world and for the more peripheral areas of Greek influence where she came to be associated with similar goddesses of other peoples. This survey has identified two particular traits that comprise Greek deities like Athena. She is the product of panhellenic notions – traits that are common throughout the Greek world. Alongside this, there were, in a sense, as many Athenas as there were Greek cities.

ATHENA AFTERWARDS

9

FROM BEING TO IMAGE: THE RISE OF CHRISTIANITY AND THE POSTCLASSICAL WORLD

'This is my favourite', he said. He held the object towards me . . . It was a little bronze statue, helmeted, clothed to the foot in carved robe with the upper incised chiton or peplum. One hand was extended as if holding a staff or rod. 'She is perfect', he said. 'Only she has lost her spear'. I did not say anything.

(HD, *Tribute to Freud*, quoted in Owen 1983: 118)

INTRODUCTION: MOVING BEYOND ANTIQUITY

Athena is one of the Greek gods who has held a special appeal since Antiquity. Her connections with civilised values, the arts, learning, justice and intelligence have given her an emblematic value second only to Aphrodite, the embodiment of sexuality and desire. Her intriguing gendered identity has helped ensure her longevity, giving her a particular prominence within feminist and psychoanalytical thinking. The symbolic potential of some of her attributes has enhanced her appeal, notably the owl and the Gorgon, both of which continue to be used as logos and emblems.

This final section will explore her postclassical image, tracing the main phases in its development from the rise of Christianity through to modern times. We will examine how, at various points, aspects of her ancient character have been adapted and transformed. It would not be feasible to do justice in a short survey to the full range of representations over two millennia; instead we will highlight some of the most notable and influential adaptations of her ancient image. Our focus will be those uses of her that have contributed to current perceptions, and some of the most notable works of literature and art in which her image has played a part. We will also look at the adoption of the goddess at key points in the history of particular states, examining the role of her image in helping to legitimise rulers and political systems.

FROM PAGAN ABOMINATION TO ETHICAL SYMBOL

While the pagan gods continued to be worshipped, Athena, like her fellow deities, was reviled by Christian authors. In their eagerness to demonstrate the superiority of Christianity, the early Christian authors sometimes adduced the Greek gods as evidence of the immorality and absurdity of paganism. Several writers employ a pre-existing list of gods, possibly part of the Aristotelian corpus, that gave them a readymade means to condemn paganism. Not only does the list highlight the worship of numerous gods instead of the one 'true' God, but some of their traits allow them to highlight the depravity of the pagan deities, Athena included. The earliest Christian writer to use this material was Clement of Alexandria, whose *Protrepticus* ('Exhortation to the Greeks') of *c.* 190 AD, adduces it as part of his denunciation of the folly of pagan worship:

> There are those who propose five Athenas: the daughter of Hephaistos, who is the Athenian; the daughter of the Nile, who is the Egyptian; a third, the daughter of Kronos, who is the inventor of war; a fourth, the daughter of Zeus, whom the Messenians call Koryphasia after her mother; above all, there is the child of Pallas and Titanis the daughter of Okeanos: having impiously sacrificed her father, she is dressed in the paternal skin just like a fleece.
>
> (2.28)

This list of five homonymous Athenas bears a curious relationship to the dominant traditions of Greek myth where Athena is almost always identified as the daughter of Zeus and Metis. The connection between a martial Athena ('the inventor of war') and Kronos is particularly difficult to account for, given that Kronos is not known for his warlike associations. The association with Hephaistos might derive from a literal interpretation of her Athenian epithet Hephaistia ('of Hephaistos'). Likewise, the assertion that Athena was called Koryphasia after her mother could perhaps derive from a literal understanding of *koryphē* ('head').

As for the fifth Athena, this goddess provides an opportunity for Clement to highlight the depravity of the gods. In this instance, the connection between Athena and a figure called Pallas is not without a parallel in Greek myth. We have already encountered other figures of this name with whom Athena has a conflict-ridden relationship: the childhood friend she accidentally killed when their war games turned nasty and the giant she defeated in the gigantomachy. The latter of these stories also involves the creation of the aegis from the flayed skin of her opponent. But, thematic parallels apart, the account of the fifth Athena involves an extraordinary inversion of the usual father–daughter relationship, replacing harmony and respect with incest, parricide and mutilation. The account produces a blend of just enough dominant and non-canonical material in order to help attack paganism.

When Constantine became Emperor in 323, Christianity became established as the leading religion of the Roman Empire. Under his sons Constans and Constantius, pagan worship was ordered to cease, with all pagan temples closed. In this climate of persecution, Firmicus Maternus wrote a treatise *On the Error of Profane Religions* (c. 346). Addressed to Constans and Constantius, it presents a sustained attack on paganism. The list of five Athenas is transformed in his work into an extended condemnation of the goddess, particularly the third and fifth homonymous goddesses:

> The third was the daughter of Saturn; they say that she was a manlike woman, for she never held herself within the modesty of the feminine sex but always remained in the midst of weapons and the din of battles, and followed the bloody excursions of war . . . the fifth is descended from her father Pallas and her mother Titanis, who, called by name after her father, is called Pallas by men. Out of her mind with parricidal fury and by the instinct of insane rashness, she cut the throat of her father Pallas in cruel death. Not content only with the death

of her father, so that she might enjoy his misfortunes all the longer, and so that she might triumph more cruelly over the death of her father, she adorned herself in the relics of his body so that she might publish her crime of parricide by cruel display.

(16.1–2)

Immodest and immoral, Athena is, for Firmicus, the epitome of pagan religion. But Firmicus was writing at a time when the threat posed by paganism to Christianity was coming to an end. His work is in the tradition of condemnatory writing, but it was somewhat outmoded in the newly Christianised world of the fourth century. The gods were beginning to adopt new roles within the Christian system of beliefs and values. Constantine had asserted his power by turning his newly created city, Constantinople, into a cultural sensation furnished with some of the greatest images of the Greek gods including Pheidias' statues of Athena Parthenos and Athena Promachos. So began a new role for Athena as a being no longer worshipped with cult, but with a place within the new system. This new role, as we shall see, was facilitated by a perceived association with the Virgin Mary.

In the early centuries of the Christian era, Mary became what Athena had been within the Greek religious system: a powerful female within a patriarchal religion. Several of Athena's cult sites, not least the Parthenon, were transformed into shrines of the Virgin Mary. Mary was also given some of the characteristics and attributes of Athena. By the fourth century, she was regularly depicted with the gorgoneion on her breast. Mary was regarded as having a warlike aspect too, as may be exemplified by a reported epiphany of the Virgin in seventh-century Constantinople. She was said to have appeared on the walls of the city when it was facing an invasion by the Avars, shaking a spear and exhorting the people. In perhaps the most striking example of a Christian saint behaving like a pagan deity, Mary adopted not only Athena's warlike characteristics, but also her role as city patron. The assimilation would have been enhanced by the transfer of the Athena Parthenos and Athena Promachos statues some three centuries earlier. This begs the question of whom the people of Constantinople would have seen when they looked at the statues: the ancient *parthenos* or the Christian Virgin. Perhaps what they would have seen is both: a paganised Mary as the new Athena.

ALLEGORY AND SYMBOLISM

Following the suppression of paganism in the fourth century AD, Athena's symbolic appeal began to be garnered by Christian thinkers. Removed from her original cultic contexts, a set of roles were created that laid the foundation for the goddess as she is principally known today.

Appropriating the ancient gods has always involved selectivity. What might be found interesting as we move through our survey is not only those aspects of the ancient goddess that have been drawn on since antiquity, but also what has been left out. Her implacability, for example, has tended to be overlooked, as has the near-malice she demonstrates in myth towards those depicted as her enemies. What has been drawn on instead are those aspects of the Greek goddess deemed more conducive to symbolism: her patronage of civilised institutions and endeavours, for example, and her support for particular cities and deserving individuals.

Athena's postclassical appeal was motivated by the ease with which she could be slotted into the Christian system of values. Her ancient associations with intelligence, craft and justice were adapted in such a way as to connect with such concepts as Justice, Prudence and above all, Wisdom. Her allegorical potential is a recurrent feature of medieval and Renaissance art. Botticelli's *Pallas and the Centaur* (1482), for example, shows the goddess taming Brute Force as represented by the Centaur. Similar ideas are presented in Mantegna's *Expulsion of the Vices from the Garden of the Virtues* (1502); the goddess is decked out in full armour driving out the Vices, interceding on behalf of the forces of good (Fortitude, Temperance, Justice) against the likes of Ignorance, Avarice, Malice and Inertia.

With the renewed interest in the arts and human endeavour that characterised the Renaissance, Athena acquired further significance

Figure 18 Luca Giodano, *Minerva as Protectress of the Arts and Sciences*, London, National Gallery L894. On loan from the collection of Sir Denis Mahon since 1999.

as a champion of the arts, learning and science, and also as a symbol of human endeavour. The goddess' continued allegorical appeal is evident in figure 18 *Minerva as Protectress of the Arts and Sciences* by Luca Giodano from the early 1680s where she is handing over the key of knowledge to Intellect, while a hammer is being given to Artifice and Industry. The myth of her birth took on fresh significance in this climate as a symbol of the emergence from the brain of God of arts and inventions. In figure 19, a seventeenth-century work by Michael Maier, Athena's birth is depicted as an alchemical achievement, with the goddess emerging out of Zeus's skull in a shower of gold while Hephaistos ('Fire') is moving his axe away from Zeus's head.

Figure 19 Athena's birth in a golden shower, Michael Maier, *Atalanta Fugiens*. Reproduced by permission of Glasgow University Library, Department of Special Collections.

Athena's symbolic potential led to her association in the sixteenth and seventeenth centuries with a succession of female rulers. In Thomas Blenerhasset's *A Revelation of the True Minerva* (1582), Elizabeth I is presented as the 'new Minerva' in whose person 'the greatest goddesse nowe on earth is seene'. Above all, the image of Athena/Minerva was used in relation to the series of female regents who emerged in France as rulers on behalf of their young sons: Catherine de' Medici (r. 1560–71), regent in the reign of Charles IX, Marie de' Medici (r. 1610–17), the regent for Louis XIII and Anne of Austria (r. 1642–52), the regent in the reign of Louis XIV. These queens were variously represented as the protégées of the goddess,

or even represented with her attributes. The image of Athena/
Minerva was particularly powerful in relation to these regents
because it helped overturn the anomaly of female rulers in a system
where women were forbidden under Salic Law from inheriting
the throne.

The appeal of the image of Athena in connection with these
regents may be exemplified by a series of paintings by Rubens of
Marie de Medici where Athena is shown as her patron. She is
helping her to read in one painting, and in another escorting her as
she escapes from Blois. In the final painting, Marie has moved from
being depicted as Athena's protégée to, practically, having become
an incarnation of the goddess. Depicted victorious in battle, Marie is
wearing a helmet, carrying a shield, holding a winged Victory, with
the spoils of war at her feet. This is almost a representation of Marie
as Athena except that she has her right breast uncovered, a detail
which has the effect of counterbalancing the warrior attributes with
maternal traits. Marie is a victorious leader; she is also a mother
ruling on behalf of her young son.

Athena was a convenient image to be used in this context,
enabling Marie to be envisaged as at once a strong and powerful
female and as well-disposed towards patriarchy. The image of
Athena provided a means of helping to legitimise her rule as a
powerful woman who would have the nation's interests at heart.
In so doing, her postclassical function as the embodiment of moral
values is being adduced, as is the classical image of the strong
female who upholds civilised, male values.

Athena's allegorical value was so pervasive that she 'survived'
the French Revolution. While statues of the other pagan gods dis-
appeared from France, as did the Christian God himself, Athena
endured as a symbol of one of the fundamental Virtues of the new
system: Liberty. A statue of the goddess stood in the Place de la
Révolution where it watched over the guillotine. Such was her
connection with French politics that her image flourished in the
aftermath of the Revolution, through her adoption as patron of the
Classe des Sciences morales et politiques, established in 1797 to
facilitate the study of culture and more broadly to provide stability
in the early post-Revolutionary years.

These examples from sixteenth-, seventeenth- and eighteenth-century France demonstrate one of the most intriguing aspects of Athena: that she is capable of being connected with particular individuals and groups while ultimately transcending any single faction. In a sense, her role in France represents a continuation of that in ancient Athens where her intimate connection with the tyrants did not preclude her from being adopted as the patron of the emergent democracy. As an image of nationhood, Athena favours prominent individuals and groups but, with her emblematic appeal, she also transcends any single faction.

So was set in place the dominant way in which Athena has been represented in Western culture. In addition to France, she has had a place in many cities. There is a statue of Athena in the Square at Budapest, for example, and outside the parliament building in Vienna. The Victoria Art Gallery in Bath is adorned with an image of the goddess and, as we have seen, there is a bust of the goddess on top of the Old Library in Cardiff (p. 3). Her image has also played a role in shaping representations of other armed females including the Statue of Liberty, symbol of the American nation, and Britannia, the figurehead of the British nation, who as a helmeted female holding an olive branch is still found on the 50p coin. Two recent uses of Athena demonstrate her continued symbolic appeal. Athena is the name of the fictional American college in Philip Roth's novel *The Human Stain* (2000). Perhaps the innovative use made of the goddess in recent years, meanwhile, is as the figurehead for the London Metropolitan Police's 'Racial and Violent Crimes Taskforce', established to combat hate crime. The name of the taskforce is 'Operation Athena', in their words 'for the Greek goddess of wisdom and the city' (www.met.police.uk/police/mps/athena/athena5.htm).

LITERARY ATHENAS

Athena's symbolic potential, combined with her paradoxical nature, has helped to inspire various literary works. This section will examine three examples, all of which draw in particular upon her birth for its potential for symbolism: Milton's *Paradise Lost* (published 1667), Roberto Calasso's *Marriage of Cadmus and Harmony* (English translation 1993) and John Banville's *Athena* (1995).

Although Athena has had a long-lasting appeal as a symbol of moral values and virtues, in *Paradise Lost*, she is the model for Sin, the daughter of Satan. The myth of her birth is among a series of ancient stories adapted by Milton to create a Christianised epic universe in which the pagan gods are models for the Fallen Angels and other beings. When Satan is making his way from Hell to earth, with a view to undermining God's newly created Adam and Eve, he comes across the 'Snakie Sorceress' (2.724) who holds the key to the gate of Hell, only to discover that the prodigy is his daughter Sin:

> Hast thou forgot me then, and do I seem
> Now in thine eye so foul, once deemed so fair
> In Heav'n, when at the' Assembly, and in sight
> Of all the Seraphim with thee combin'd
> In bold conspiracy against Heav'ns King,
> All on a sudden miserable pain
> Surpris'd thee, dim thine, eyes, and dizzie swumm
> In darkness, while thy head flames thick and fast
> Threw forth, till on the left side op'ning wide,
> Likest to thee in shape and count'nance fair, a Goddess armd
> Out of thy head I sprung: amazement seiz'd
> All th' Host of Heav'n; back they recoild afraid
> At first, and called me *Sin*, and for a Sign
> Portentous held me.

(747–61)

Sin's birth contains echoes of Athena's emergence to the astonishment of the assembled gods in *Homeric Hymn* 28 (Chapter 1). Again like Athena, Sin develops a particular relationship with her father except that Milton depicts an incestuous relationship between them:

> familiar grown,
> I pleas'd, and with attractive glances won
> The most averse, thee chiefly, who full oft

Thy self in me thy perfet image viewing
Becam'st enamour'd, and such joy thou tookst
With me in secret.

(761–6)

One of the most salient features of Athena's ancient persona, her intimate relationship with her father, is rendered so close by Milton that it becomes incestuous.

From seventeenth-century epic we move to two late twentieth-century novels, first Roberto Calasso's retelling of classical mythology, *The Marriage of Cadmus and Harmony*. Calasso draws on a range of myths, using as a focal point the abduction of Europa by Zeus and her brother Cadmus' marriage to Harmony. We meet Athena early on when she looks down from heaven to see her father in the form of a bull with a girl on his back and 'blushed at the sight of her father bestraddled by a girl' (3). The virgin Athena is at this stage envisaged as embarrassed at her father's sexual activity. Later the story of her is related in a way that focuses on the closeness, the oneness even, between father and daughter. When Zeus swallowed Metis 'the baby girl had flowed into Zeus's body' (225), her femininity concealed behind her weapons:

Everything about that little girl was sharp: her eyes, her mind – now living in the mind of her father – the point of her helmet. Every female concavity was hidden away, like the reverse side of her shield.

(225)

The sense of 'oneness' with her father is envisaged as close to incestuous after she had been born:

Athena had appeared in the crack on his skull, her weapons sparkling, while Nike fluttered around her with a crown in her hand.

Now he could see her too: she was walking away from her father. Turning her head in silent greeting, she was the only one who looked him in the eyes. Was it his daughter he saw, or his own image gazing back at him?

(226)

But while in a sense a duplicate of her father, she is also envisaged as a separate being, whose first task on being born is to divest herself of her weapons:

> Athena was the only being who, at birth, did not grab at something but took something off . . . She put down her shield, her helmet, her javelin; she undid the aegis . . . she set off towards Lake Tritonis. There she immersed herself in the water, as if to renew a virginity she would never lose. But she had a far deeper intimacy to break away from: the fact that she had been mingled with the body of her father.
>
> (226)

In a way that parallels Milton's account of the birth of Sin, the intimacy between father and daughter is so close that there is something incestuous about it. When Clement and Firmicus discussed Athena in the early Christian centuries it was also incest that was emphasised. This points us to a recurrent feature of representations of Athena's father–daughter relationships outside the confines of paganism. In Greek religion, her relationship with her father expressed the respective place of herself and Zeus within the pantheon. Divested of its religious framework, what is left is an image of familial love that verges on the perverse.

John Banville's *Athena* is the third novel in a trilogy also comprising *The Book of Evidence* (1989) and *Ghosts* (1993) involving the art critic Freddie Montgomery, who has taken on the name Morrow. Having spent time in prison for the murder of a young woman, the third novel deals with his love affair with another young woman, a disturbed and elusive woman only ever given the name 'A'. The novel sees Morrow looking back over the relationship with A in ways that frequently allude to the figure and myth of Athena. A recurrent theme is Athena's birth, in which Morrow is characterised as Zeus and A as Athena. Early on, he is 'holding you in my head' (1), while A herself is 'poised to leap . . . like one lingering on the brink of departure' (2). As he begins to embark on his narrative, 'a crack in my mind jumps in panic' (3). He has been suffering from headaches (e.g. 4).

Meanwhile, Morrow has been commissioned to describe a series of paintings on classical mythological topics by Dutch Masters, the final one of which depicts the birth of Athena by one named Jean Vaublin:

> Consider these creatures, these people who are not people, these inhabitants of heaven. The god has a headache, his son wields the axe, the girl springs forth, with bow and shield. She is walking towards the world. Her owl flies before her. It is twilight. Look at these clouds, this limitless and impenetrable sky. This is what remains . . . Everything is changed and yet the same.
>
> (232)

The motif of Athena's birth captures the intensity of the relationship between Morrow and A while depicting it as something transient, with the girl always on the brink of departure. It also presents the relationship as something perverse, with the age difference between Morrow and A as a near father–daughter relationship. In Banville's novel, the birth of Athena is envisaged as at once pain-inducing and creative. With this duality, it serves as a model for the relationship between Morrow and A, which, unhealthy and temporary though it is, is at the same time inspirational. *Athena*, together with the other two works examined in this section demonstrates the continued fascination with the myth of Athena's birth as something intriguing and strange, establishing a uniquely intimate relationship between father and daughter, one that is to varying degrees presented as incestuous.

FEMINISM AND GENDER THEORY

With her unique blend of feminine and masculine attributes and concerns, Athena has generated a range of responses in writing about gender and in feminist scholarship. A little bronze statuette of Athena was among the most treasured items in Freud's personal collection (see the passage quoted at the head of this chapter). The goddess encapsulated to some degree his theory of gender. In a manuscript dated to 1922, he represents Medusa's head as a symbol of castration, with her appeal as an image deriving from male anxiety:

This symbol of horror is worn upon her dress by the virgin goddess Athena. And rightly so, for thus she becomes a woman who is unapproachable and repels all sexual desires – since she displays the terrifying genitals of the Mother.

(1981: 274)

In feminist writing, a 'split' may be discerned as regards how to read the image of Athena. For some, she is an empowering figure, who embodies the potential for female power within patriarchy. For others, she is the ultimate patriarchal sell out: the strong woman who uses her powers to promote and advance men rather than others of her sex.

Bachofen established an image of Athena that has been enduringly popular since the publication of his *Das Mutterrecht* in the nineteenth century. It was here, as we saw in Chapter 2, that Athena was presented as the agent of 'father-right', whose support for Orestes and pacification of the furies helped inaugurate the 'age of Apollo', the new system dominated by the Olympian gods and by human males. For Bachofen, Athena's intervention on behalf of patriarchy marked a necessary development in human progress. In subsequent scholarship, his ideas have been embraced, but with a feminist spin. The primordial matriarchy he sets out is seen instead as a golden age, an ideal to be celebrated. This feminist reinterpretation has seen a re-evaluation of Athena's role in the transition to patriarchy. In the early twentieth century, as we have seen (Chapter 2), Jane Harrison envisaged Athena as a patriarchal 'sell out', the 'Lost Leader' who became through her collusion with the male anomalous and even unlikeable: 'we cannot love a goddess who on principle forgets the Earth from which she sprang' (1903: 303–4). Comparable ideas are presented in more recent writing. The French feminist/psychoanalysist Luce Irigaray has identified something 'still extremely contemporary' in Athena's promotion of Orestes. 'Here and there', she writes, 'regulation Athenas whose one begetter is the head of the Father King still burst forth . . . completely in his pay' (Irigaray 1991: 37). Adrienne Rich, meanwhile, in a speech to women at the all-female Smith College, warned young women against being taken in by 'the myth of the "special" woman, the unmothered Athena sprung from her father's brow' (1985: 121).

Other feminist writers, meanwhile, have taken reassurance from Athena's patriarchal affinities, even going so far as to reclaim the goddess as a symbol of strong femininity. Christine Downing has discussed her own life and career as a woman/academic in relation to her changing 'relationship' with Athena. She recounts how her evolving interpretation of the goddess helped her come to terms with the tension involved in being an intelligent woman within a male-dominated world (1981). Anne Shearer's Jungian study of the goddess, meanwhile, has given precedence to Athena's female, and, even, gynocentric, traits, seeing in her the archetypal image of ancient female power, rather than solely an instrument of Zeus or of patriarchy. As such, according to Shearer, she 'ensures that the ancient feminine is honoured in the very seat of patriarchal power' (1996: 59).

This feminist appropriation of Athena has a parallel in several 'Athena Projects' established in the late twentieth century, each of which aims to promote female participation in traditionally male fields such as mathematics, science and technology. One of these, the 'Athena Project', was launched in 1999 to promote women in science, technology and engineering in Higher Education in the United Kingdom. In the US, meanwhile, 'Project Athena', based in California, was set up to help further educational opportunities for young women in mathematics and science. Another 'Athena Project', an initiative in Washington State, was established to develop science, mathematics and technology in schools. These innovations continue a notable tradition connecting Athena with women's educational establishments, including Bedford College in London and, above all, Bryn Mawr College in Pennsylvania. A copy of the Athena Lemnia (figure 9) has been in the possession of the College since 1906. In its current home, the Thomas Building, students even 'worship' the goddess, leaving offerings and requests for help in their academic endeavours.

The 'split' within feminism over how to interpret Athena enables us to emphasise once again the duality of the goddess. As a strong female who rejects male domination and is a powerful figure in the male-dominated world of the ancient Greeks, she has been embraced as a symbol of female empowerment. For others, meanwhile, she is the traitor to her sex who colludes in the oppression of women.

OVERVIEW

So ends our survey of Athena. No single modern version of the goddess has emerged. As we might expect of an ancient deity characterised by her multifaceted nature, her image has been used in a variety of ways over the centuries. First adopted as a kind of precursor of the Virgin Mary, she was subsequently worked into the Christianised system of values, with her connections with intelligence and craft making her viable as an ethical symbol. Her role as the patron of cities and civic institutions has been drawn on in various modern contexts, so much so that images of Athena are now to be found in the public art of numerous Western cities. Her distinctive blend of masculine and feminine attributes has helped ensure a continued role within feminist thinking. Her distorted femininity has been used variously to illustrate the subordination of women and as an empowering image for women operating in traditionally male fields.

FURTHER READING

This guide will list a range of works, with particular concentration on those that pertain to material discussed in this book. A more extensive bibliography of works dealing with Athena is contained in Deacy and Villing (2001b).

WHY ATHENA?

For a brief introductory overview, see Parker's (1996a) entry in the *Oxford Classical Dictionary*, reprinted in Price and Kearns (2003), 68–70. A succinct introduction to the goddess is provided in Burkert (1985), 139–43. Athena's image in art is covered in the *Athena* entry in the *Lexicon Iconographicum Mythologiae Classicae* (Demargne 1984). Of Athena's attributes, the aegis has come in for extensive discussion. Recent discussions include Vierck (1997) and Robertson (2001). The Internet is a mine of information, although as with any topic in Greek religion and mythology, some sites should be approached with caution. The most extensive online resource is *The Shrine of the Goddess Athena* (http://www.goddess-athena.org/). Myths connected with Athena are retold for children in Woff's enjoyable book (1999).

THE BIRTH OF ATHENA

The two major works on Near-Eastern influences upon Greek culture are Burkert (1992) and West (1999). Mesopotamian antecedents of the story of Athena's birth are explored in Penglase (1994), especially chapter 10. On frontality, see Frontisi-Ducroux (1989). Athena's connection with Zeus is examined in Sydinou (1986) and Neils (2001b). The succession myth, especially the Hesiodic version, has been the subject of extensive discussion. See e.g. Detienne and Vernant (1978), 107–30 and from a gendered perspective, Arthur (1982), Doherty (1995), 1–8 and Thomas (1998).

TRACING ATHENA'S ORIGINS

Critiques of the 'Goddess theory' are presented in Goodison and Morris (1998) and Eller (2000). Athena's role in the *Oresteia*, including her relationship with Klytaimnestra, is explored in Goldhill (1992). On Bernal's derivation of Athena from Neith, see e.g. Jasanoff and Nussbaum (1996). Bernal (2001) is a response to their criticisms. Teffeteller (2001) deals with the similarities between Athena and the Hittite sun goddess of Arinna. The potential of Indo-European scholarship to shed light upon Athena's origins is demonstrated by Allen's (2001) comparison of Athena's interventions in the *Odyssey* with that of the Hindu goddess Durgā in the *Mahābhārata*.

FROM ORIGINS TO FUNCTIONS: ATHENA IN THE PANTHEON

Structuralist-influenced or 'Paris School' studies that have examined Athena include Detienne (1971–2), Detienne and Vernant (1978, esp. section IV) and Darmon (1991). The structuralist opposition between Athena and Ares is assessed in Deacy (2000). Athena's role as a maritime deity is explored in relation to her connection with promontories in Robertson (1996). An unusual perspective on Athena's warrior persona is presented in Milanezi (2001), who considers her connections with laughter. Another of her spheres of influence are explored in Serghidou (2001), which looks particularly at her connections with the aulos and the salpinx (war trumpet).

HEROES, HEROINES AND THE TROJAN WAR

Athena's relationships with various heroes in drama are considered in Papadopoulou (2001), notably Herakles and Ajax. Medea's role as the helper of Jason is explored in Griffiths (2005), 35–6. On the Athena-Odysseus relationship, see Clay (1983) and Pucci (1987). Deacy (2005) explores Athena's relationship with Herakles. The goddess' connections with epic heroism is investigated by Spence (2001) via an examination of the role of Pallas in the *Aeneid*.

ATHENA IN ATHENS: PATRON, SYMBOL AND 'MOTHER'

The nature of Athenian religion is examined in book length form in the major study by Parker (2005). Deacy (2007) provides a chapter-long account. The Akropolis in Athenian history and myth is explored in Hurwit (1999). Athena's role in Athenian literature, including Solon fragment 4, is explored in Herington (1963). On the myth of Erichthonios, see Parker (1987), Loraux (1993) and Deacy (1997a). The sources are conveniently assembled in Powell (1906). On the Chalkeia, see Simon (1983), 38–9. Studies of the Arrhephoria include Robertson (1983), Boedeker (1984) and Rosenzweig (2004), 45–58. On the Hephaisteion, a joint temple to Athena and Hephaistos, see Harrison (1997a), (1997b) and (1997c). The place of Athena in the religious life of the city as it emerges from dedications on the Akropolis discussed in Wagner (2001). An interesting perspective is offered in Karanika (2001), which examines the potential of Homeric epic to elucidate religious practice notably the Panathenaia. The iconography of Athena on Athenian vases is considered in Villing (1992) [2007].

EARLY ATHENIAN HISTORY

Athena's possible connections with the Mycenaean Akropolis are discussed in Hurwit (1999), 13–14, 67–84. On the two Homeric references to Athena and Erechtheus, see Parker (1996b), 19–20. The period 600–480 is examined in Hurwit (1999), 99–136. On the Panathenaia, see Neils (1992) and Neils (1996). The transformation of Athenian cult under the Peisistratids is explored in Shapiro (1989). On Peisistratos' chariot ride with Phye, see Connor (1987) and Sinos (1993). The popularity of Herakles in sixth-century Athens is considered in Boardman (1972). On coins of Athena under the Peisistratids, see van der Vin (2000).

ALL ABOUT ATHENA? THE CLASSICAL AKROPOLIS

The classical Akropolis is examined in Hurwit (1999), 138–245 and Hurwit (2004). Gendered images presented on the Parthenon are explored in Blundell (1998). The Amazons and their relationship to Athena are considered in Deacy (1997b). Studies of the Parthenon include Beard (2002) and Neils (2005). Connelly's theory on the frieze is presented in Connelly (1996). Other accounts of the frieze and its interpretation include Jenkins (1994) and Neils (2001a). There is an insightful overview in Woodford (2003), 220–9. On the statue of Athena Parthenos, see Leipen (1971). The body of the goddess as represented in classical Athenian art is investigated by Llewellyn-Jones (2001). Loraux (1992) raises interpretative issues pertaining to the study of Greek goddesses, Athena included. Representations of Athena from the fourth century onwards are explored in Altripp (2001) and (2007).

THE WIDER GREEK WORLD

The major study of Athena cults across the Greek world is Villing (1998a). Athena's cult at Sparta is discussed in Villing (1997). The 'mystery' of the bells is the topic of Villing (2002). On Argos and Kallimachos' *Bath of Pallas*, see most recently Morrison (2005).

Studies of the sanctuary of Athena Alea include Voyatzis (1990) and Voyatzis (1998). Discussions of other sites include Corinth in Ritter (2001) and Villing (1997), Stymphalos in Williams and Schaus (2001), Lindos in Higbie (2001), Pergamon in Faita (2001), Priene in Carter (1983) and Ptolemaic Egypt in Mathiopoulos (2001). Athena's Boiotian cult is discussed in Schachter (1981) and Deacy (1995). The east Greek world is examined in Villing (1998b) and Işik (2004). Athena's relationship with Minerva is explored in Graf (2001).

THE RISE OF CHRISTIANITY AND THE POSTCLASSICAL WORLD

The image of Athena from antiquity onwards is surveyed in Warner (1996) and Shearer (1996). Some of the main trends in representations and scholarship are examined in Deacy and Villing (2001a). The use of Athena in early Christianity is considered in Shearer (1996), chapters 6 and 7. On the epiphany of Mary/Athena in Constantinople, see Grosby (1996). The allegorical appeal of Athena in the postclassical world is surveyed in Shearer (1996), chapter 8. On Mantegna's *Expulsion of the Vices from the Garden of the Virtues* see Warner (1996), 151–2. Athena's image in relation to the arts, learning and science is addressed in Spaanstra-Polak (1973).

Female rulers, including Marie de Medici, are discussed in May (1984). On Marie de Medici, see further Thuillier (1970). On the image of Athena/Minerva in post-revolutionary France, see Staum (1996). Britannia's connection with Athena is explored in Warner (1996), 47–8. Another aspect of Athena's reception, her appropriation by the artists of the Secession Movement in Vienna in the turn of the nineteenth and twentieth centuries (including Klimt and Stuck) is explored in Karentzos (2001).

Freud's ideas about Medusa in his manuscript of 1922 are contained in Freud (1981). The applicability of psychoanalysis to the study of Greek myth is explored in Doherty (2001) chapter 2. Downing (1981) and Shearer (1996) present feminist reappraisals of Athena. Her less 'empowering' aspects are considered in Irigaray (1991, 37).

WORKS CITED

Allen, N. (2001), 'Athena and Durgā: Warrior Goddesses in Greek and Sanskrit Epic', in Deacy and Villing (2001), 367–82.

Altripp, I. (2001), 'Small Athenas: Some Remarks on Late Classical and Hellenistic Statues', in Deacy and Villing (2001), 181–95.

—— (2007), *Athenastatuen der Spätklassik und des Hellenismus*, Cologne and Weimar.

Arthur, M.B. (1982), 'Cultural Strategies in Hesiod's *Theogony*', *Arethusa* 15, 63–82.

Atwood, M. (1976), *Lady Oracle*, Toronto.

Bachofen, J.J. (1967), 'Mother Right: An Investigation of the Religious and Juridical Character of Matriarchy in the Ancient World', in *Myth, Religion and Mother Right: Selected Writings*, London, 67–207.

Banville, J. (1995), *Athena*, London.

—— (1989), *The Book of Evidence*, London.

—— (1993), *Ghosts*, London.

Baring, A. and Cashford, J. (1991), *The Myth of the Goddess: Evolution of an Image*, London.

Beard, M. (2002), *The Parthenon*, London.

Bernal, M. (2001), *Black Athena Writes Back: Martin Bernal Responds to his Critics*, Durham and London.

Blundell, S. (1998), 'Marriage and the Maiden: Narratives on the Parthenon', in Blundell, S. and Williamson, M. (eds), *The Sacred and the Feminine in Ancient Greece*, London and New York, 47–70.

Boardman, J. (1972), 'Herakles, Peisistratos and Sons', *Revue Archéologique* 57–72.

Boedeker, D.D. (1984), *Descent from Heaven: Images of Dew in Greek Poetry and Religion*, Chico, Calif.

Burkert, W. (1985), *Greek Religion: Archaic and Classical*, Oxford.

—— (1992), *The Orientalizing Revolution: Near Eastern Influence on Greek Culture in the Early Archaic Age*, Cambridge, Mass.

Calasso, R. (1993), *The Marriage of Cadmus and Harmony*, London.

Carpenter, T.H. (1991), *Art and Myth in Ancient Greece*, London.

Carter, J.C. (1983), *The Sculpture of the Sanctuary of Athena Polias at Priene*, London.

Clay, J.S. (1983), *The Wrath of Athena: Gods and Men in the* Odyssey, Princeton.

Connelly, J.B. (1996), 'Parthenon and *Parthenoi*: A Mythological Interpretation of the Parthenon Frieze', *American Journal of Archaeology* 100, 53–80.

Connor, W.R. (1987), 'Tribes, Festivals and Processions: Civic Ceremonial and Political Manipulation in Archaic Greece', *Journal of Hellenic Studies* 107, 40–50.

Cook, A.B. (1914–40), *Zeus: A Study in Ancient Religion*, Cambridge, 3 vols., in 5 parts.

Daraki, M. (1980), 'Le héros à *menos* et le héros *daimoni isos*: une polarité homerique', *Annali della Scuola Normale Superiore de Pisa*, 10, 1–24.

Darmon, J.-P. (1991), 'The Powers of War: Ares and Athena in Greek Mythology', in Bonnefoy, Y. (ed.), *Greek and Egyptian Mythologies*, Chicago and London, 114–15.

Deacy, S.J. (1995), 'Athena in Boiotia: Local Tradition and Cultural Identity' in Fossey, J. (ed.), *Boiotia Antiqua V: Studies on Boiotian Topography, Cults and Terracottas*, Amsterdam, 91–103.

—— (1997a), 'The Vulnerability of Athena: Parthenoi and Rape in Greek Myth' in Deacy, S.J. and Pierce, K.F. (eds), *Rape in Antiquity: Sexual Violence in the Greek and Roman Worlds*, London, 43–63.

—— (1997b), 'Athena and the Amazons: Mortal and Immortal Femininity in Greek Myth', in Lloyd, A.B. (ed.), *What is a God? Studies in the Nature of Greek Divinity*, London, 285–98.

—— (2000), 'Athena and Ares: War, Violence and Warlike Deities', in van Wees, H. (ed.), *War and Violence in Ancient Greece*, London and Swansea, 285–98.

—— (2005) 'Herakles and his "Girl": Heroism, Athena and Beyond', in Rawlings, L. and Bowden, H. (ed.), *Herakles and Hercules: Exploring a Graeco-Roman Deity*, Swansea, 37–50.

—— (2007), ' "Famous Athens, Divine Polis": the Religious System in Athens' in Ogden, D. (ed.), *A Companion to Greek Religion*, Oxford, 221–35.

Deacy, S.J. and Villing, A.C. (2001) *Athena in the Classical World*, Leiden, Boston and Cologne.

—— (2001a), 'Athena Past and Present: An Introduction', in Deacy and Villing (2001), 1–25.

—— (2001b), 'Bibliography of Work Pertaining to Athena', in Deacy and Villing (2001), 383–95.

Demargne, P. (and Cassimatis, H.) (1984), 'Athena', in *Lexicon Iconographicum Mythologiae Classicae* 2, Munich and Zurich, 955–1044.

Detienne, M. (1971–2), 'Athena and the Mastery of the Horse', *History of Religions* 11, 161–84.

Detienne, M. and Vernant, J.-P. (1978), *Cunning Intelligence in Greek Culture and Society*, Brighton.

Doherty, L.E. (1995), *Siren Songs. Gender, Audiences, and Narrators in the Odyssey*, Ann Arbor.

—— (2001), *Gender and the Interpretation of Classical Myth*, London.

Dougherty, C. (2005), *Prometheus*, London and New York.

Dowden, K. (2006), *Zeus*, London and New York.

Downing, C. (1981), 'Dear Grey Eyes: A Revaluation of Pallas Athene', *Southern Humanities Review* 15.2, 97–118.

Eller, C. (2000), *The Myth of Matriarchal Prehistory: Why an Invented Past Won't Give Women a Future*, Boston.

Faita, A.S. (2001), 'The Medusa-Athena Nikephoros Coin from Pergamon', in Deacy and Villing (2001), 163–79.

Farnell, L.R. (1896–1909), *The Cults of the Greek States*, Oxford, 5 vols.

Freud, S. (1981), 'Medusa's Head', in *Standard Edition of the Complete Psychological Works*, vol. 18, *Beyond the Pleasure Principle, Group Psychology and Other Works, 1920–22*, London, 273–4.

Frontisi-Ducroux, F. (1989), 'In the Mirror of the Mask', in Bérard, C. et al., *A City of Images: Iconography and Society in Ancient Greece*, Princeton, 151–65.

Goldhill, S. (1992), *Aeschylus: The Oresteia*, Cambridge.

Goodison, L. and Morris, C. (1998), *Ancient Goddesses: The Myths and the Evidence*, London.

Graf, F. (2001), 'Athena and Minerva: Two Faces of One Goddess?', in Deacy and Villing (2001), 127–39.

Griffiths, E. (2005), *Medea*, London.

Grosby, S. (1996), 'The Category of the Primordial in the Study of Early Christianity and Second-Century Judaism', *History of Religions* (36), 140–63.

Hall, E. (1996), 'When is a Myth Not a Myth? Bernal's "Ancient Model"', in Lefkowitz, M.R. and Rogers, G.M. (eds), *Black Athena Revisited*, Chapel Hill and London, 333–48.

Harrison, E.B. (1977a), 'Alalkamenes' Sculptures for the Hephaisteion: Part I. The Cult Statues', *American Journal of Archaeology* 81, 137–78.

—— (1977b), 'Alalkamenes' Sculptures for the Hephaisteion: Part II. The Base', *American Journal of Archaeology* 81, 265–87.

—— (1977c), 'Alalkamenes' Sculptures for the Hephaisteion: Part III. Iconography and Style', *American Journal of Archaeology* 81, 411–26.

Harrison, J.E. (1903), *Prolegomena to the Study of Greek Religion*, Cambridge.

Hegel, G.W.F. (1956) [1899], *Philosophy of History*, New York.

Herington, C.J. (1955), *Athena Parthenos and Athena Polias: A Study in the Religion of Periclean Athens*, Manchester.

—— (1963), 'Athena in Athenian Literature and Cult', in Hooker, G.T.W. (ed.), *Parthenos and Parthenon*, Oxford, 61–73.

Higbie, C. (2001), 'Homeric Athena in the Chronicle of Lindos', in Deacy and Villing (2001), 105–25.

Hurwit, J. (1999), *The Athenian Acropolis*, Cambridge.

—— (2004), *The Acropolis in the Age of Pericles*, Cambridge.

Irigaray, L. (1991), 'The Bodily Encounter with the Mother', in Whitford, M., *Luce Irigaray: Philosophy in the Feminine*, London and New York, 34–46.

Işik, F. (2004), 'Zur anatolischen Athena im Lichte der Athena Ergane von Ilion under der Athena Nikephoros von Pergamon', *Istanbuler Mitteilungen* 54, 507–18.

Jasanoff, J. and Nussbaum, A. (1996), 'Word Games: The Linguistic Evidence in *Black Athena*', in Lefkowitz, M.R. and Rogers, G.M. (eds), *Black Athena Revisited*, Chapel Hill and London, 177–205.

Jenkins, I.D. (1994), *The Parthenon Frieze*, London.

Just, R. (1989), *Women in Athenian Law and Life*, London and New York.

Karanika, A. (2001), 'Memories of Poetic Discourse in Athena's Cult Practices', in Deacy and Villing (2001), 277–91.

Karentzos, A. (2001), 'Femininity and "Neur Mythos": Pallas Athena in Turn of the Century Art', in Deacy and Villing (2001), 259–73.

Leduc, C. (1996), 'Athéna et Héraklès: une parenté botanique?', in Jourdain-Annequin, C. and Bonnet, C. (eds), *IIᵉ Rencontre Héracléenne: Héraklès, les femmes et le féminine*, Brussels, 259–66.

Leipen, N. (1971), *Athena Parthenos: A Reconstruction*, Ontario.

Llewellyn-Jones, Ll. (2001), 'Sexy Athena: The Dress and Erotic Representation of a Virgin War-Goddess', in Deacy and Villing (2001), 233–57.

Loraux, N. (1992), 'What is a Goddess?', in Schmitt Pantel, P. (ed.), *A History of Women in the West 1, From Ancient Goddesses to Christian Saints*, Cambridge, Mass. and London, 11–44, 481–9.

—— (1993), *The Children of Athena: Athenian Ideas about Citizenship and the Division Between the Sexes* (Princeton).

Mathiopoulos, E. (2001), 'On the Transformation of the Athena Velletri Type in Hellenistic Alexandria', in Deacy and Villing (2001), 197–217.

May, L.A. (1984), *Above Her Sex: The Enigma of the Athena Parthenos in Popular Religion. Visible Religion* 3, Leiden, 106–30.

Milanezi, S. (2001), 'Headaches and Gnawed *Peplos*: Laughing With Athena', in Deacy and Villing (2001), 311–29.

Millett, K. (1971), *Sexual Politics*, London.

Morrison, A.D. (2005), 'Sexual Ambiguity and the Identity of the Narrator in Callimachus' *Hymn to Athena*', *Bulletin of the Institute of Classical Studies* 48, 27–46.

Neils, J. (ed.) (1992), *Goddess and Polis: the Panathenaic Festival in Ancient Athens*, Hanover/Princeton.

—— (ed.) (1996), *Worshipping Athena: Panathenaia and Parthenon* (Madison).

—— (2001a), *The Parthenon Frieze*, Cambridge.

—— (2001b), 'Athena: Alter Ego of Zeus', in Deacy and Villing, 2001, 219–32.

—— ed. (2005), *The Parthenon: From Antiquity to the Present*, Cambridge.

Nilsson, M.P. (1925), *A History of Greek Religion*, Oxford.

Otto, W.F. (1954), *The Homeric Gods*, New York.

Owen, U. (ed.) (1983), *Fathers: Reflections by Daughters*, London.

Papadopoulou, T. (2001), 'Representations of Athena in Greek Tragedy', in Deacy and Villing (2001), 293–31.

Parker, R.C.T. (1987), 'Myths of Early Athens' in Bremmer, J.N. (ed.), *Interpretations of Greek Mythology*, London and Sydney, 187–214.

—— (1996a), 'Athena', in Hornblower, S. and Spawforth, A.J.S. (eds), *The Oxford Classical Dictionary*, 3rd edn, Oxford, 201–2.

—— (1996b), *Athenian Religion: A History*, Oxford.

—— (2005), *Polytheism and Society at Athens*, Oxford.

Penglase, C. (1994), *Greek Myths and Mesopotamia*, London and New York.

Polignac, F., de (1995), *Cults, Territory and the Origins of the Greek City-State*, trans. J. Lloyd. Chicago.

Powell, B. (1906), *Erichthonius and the Three Daughters of Cecrops*, Ithaca.

Price, S. and Kearns, E. (2003), *The Oxford Dictionary of Classical Myth & Religion* (Oxford).

Pucci, P. (1987), *Odysseus Polutropos: Intertextual Readings in the* Odyssey *and the* Iliad, Ithaca and London.

Rehak, P. (1984), 'New Observations on the Mycenean Warrior Goddess', *Archäologischer Anzeiger*, 535–45.

Rich, A. (1985), 'Commencement address at Smith College, 1979', in Dorenkamp, A.G. et al. (eds), *Images of Women in American Popular Culture*, San Diego and London.

Ritter, S. (2001), 'Athena in Archaic Corinth: the Creation of an Iconography', in Deacy and Villing (2001), 143–62.

Robertson, N. (1983), 'The Riddle of the Arrhephoria at Athens', *Harvard Studies in Classical Philology* 8, 241–88.

—— (1996), 'Athena and Early Greek Society: Palladium Shrines and Promontory Shrines', in Dillon, M. (ed.), *Religion in the Ancient World: New Approaches*, Amsterdam, 383–475.

—— (2001), 'Athena as Weather Goddess: the *Aigis* in Myth and Ritual', in Deacy and Villing (2001), 29–55.

Rosenzweig, R. (2004), *Worshipping Aphrodite: Art and Cult in Classical Athens*, Ann Arbor.

Roth, P. (2000), *The Human Stain*, London.

Ruskin, J. (1890), *The Queen of the Air: Being a Study of the Greek Myths of Cloud and Storm*, Orpington and London.

Schachter, A. (1981), *Cults of Boiotia 1: Acheloos to Hera*, London, *sv. Athena*.

Serghidou, A. (2001), 'Athena *Salpinx* and the Ethics of Music', in Deacy and Villing (2001), 57–74.

Shapiro, H.A. (1989), *Art and Cult under the Tyrants in Athens*, Mainz.

Shearer, A. (1996), *Athene: Image and Energy*, London.

Simon, E. (1983), *Festivals of Attica: An Archaeological Commentary*, Madison.

Sinos, R. (1993), 'Divine Selection: Epiphany and Politics in Archaic Greece' in Dougherty, C. and Kurke, L. (eds), *Cultural Poetics in Archaic Greece: Cult, Performance, Politics*, New York and Oxford, 73–91.

Sourvinou-Inwood, C. (1993), 'Early Sanctuaries, the Eighth Century and Ritual Space: Fragments of a Discourse', in Marinatos, N. and Hägg, R. (eds), *Greek Sanctuaries: New Approaches*, London, 1–17.

Spaanstra-Polak, B. (1973), 'The Birth of Athena: An Emblematic Representation', in Bruyn, J., Emmens, J. et al. (eds), *Album Amicorum J.G. van Gelder*, The Hague, 293–305.

Spence, S. (2001), Pallas/Athena in and out of the *Aeneid*, in Deacy and Villing (2001), 331–47.

Staum, M.S. (1996), *Minerva's Message: Stabilizing the French Revolution*, Montreal and London.

Sydinou, K. (1986), 'The Relationship between Zeus and Athena in the *Iliad*', *Dodone* 15.2, 155–64.

Teffeteller, A. (2001), 'Greek Athena and the Hittite Sungoddess of Arinna', in Deacy and Villing, 2001, 349–65.

Thomas, L. (1998), 'Fathers as Mothers: the Myth of Male Parthenogenesis', in Spass, L. (ed.), *Paternity and Fatherhood: Myths and Realities*, London, 204–18.

Thuillier, J. (1970), *Rubens'* Life of Marie de' Medici, New York.

van der Vin, J.P.A. (2000), 'Coins at the time of Peisistratos', in Sancisi-Weerdenburg, H., *Peisistratos and the Tyranny: A Reappraisal of the Evidence*, Amsterdam.

Vernant, J.-P. (1979), *Myth and Society in Ancient Greece*, Brighton.

—— (1991), *Mortals and Immortals: Collected Essays*, Princeton.

Vierck, S. (1997), 'Aegis' in *Lexicon Iconographicum Mythologiae Classicae* 8, Munich and Zurich, 510–15.

Villing, A.C. (1992) [2007] *The Iconography of Athena in Attic Vase-painting from 440–370* BC, MPhil thesis, University of Oxford. Published online at <http://archiv.ub.uni-heidelberg.de/propylaeumdok/volltexte/2007/36/>.

—— (1997), 'Aspects of Athena in the Greek Polis: Sparta and Corinth', in Lloyd, A.B. (ed.), *What is a God? Studies in the Nature of Greek Divinity*, London, 81–100.

—— (1998a), *The Iconography of Athena in Mainland Greece and the East Greek World in the Fifth and Fourth Centuries* BC, DPhil thesis, University of Oxford.

—— (1998b), 'Athena as Ergane and Promachos: The Iconography of Athena in Archaic East Greece', in van Wees, H. (ed.), *Archaic Greece: New Approaches and New Evidence*, London, 147–68.

—— (2002), 'For Whom did the Bell Toll in Ancient Greece? Archaic and Classical Greek Bells at Sparta and Beyond', *Annual of the British School at Athens* 97, 223–96.

Voyatzis, M. (1990), *The Early Sanctuary of Athena Alea at Tegea*, Gothenburg.

—— (1998), 'From Athena to Zeus: An A–Z Guide to the Origins of Greek Goddesses', in Goodison, L. and Morris, C. (eds), *Ancient Goddesses: The Myths and the Evidence*, London, 133–47.

Wagner, C. (2001), 'The Worship of Athena on the Athenian Acropolis: Dedications of Plaques and Plates', in Deacy and Villing (2001), 95–104.

Warner, M. (1996), *Monuments and Maidens: The Allegory of the Female Form*, London.

West, M.L. (1999), *The East Face of Helicon: West Asiatic Elements in Greek Poetry and Myth*, Oxford.

West, M.L. (1983), *The Orphic Poems*, Oxford.

Williams, H. and Schaus, G. (2001), 'The Sanctuary of Athena at Ancient Stymphalos', in Deacy and Villing (2001), 75–94.

Woff, R. (1999), *Bright-Eyed Athena in the Myths of Ancient Greece*, London.

Wolff, V. (1982), *The Diary of Virginia Woolf, vol. 4 1931–1935*, London.

Woodford, S. (2003), *Images of Myths in Classical Antiquity*, Cambridge.

INDEX

Many Greek names are transcribed as written in Greek (e.g. -os endings and k rather than c). Latin spellings have been adopted for words that have come to be naturalised in their Latinised forms (e.g. Oedipus rather than Oidipous).

Printed in the USA/Agawam, MA
December 19, 2014

603877.032